Praise for *Being Agile in Business*

'Great, practical and comprehensive. Learn how to apply the agile mindset
directly to your business and see it flourish.'
n Floryan, Tech Lead, comparethemarket.com

a wide range of useful and modern techniques. It's an inspirational
al for any business leader!'
arritt, Principal Consultant, ThoughtWorks

t-read for anyone considering adopting agile, it will significantly speed
"aha" moments.'
and, IBM and agile practitioner

oyable read from cover to cover on the core practices and benefits of
gile.'
n Hughes, Group Program Manager, Client frameworks, Skype

o use agile in any business. Every business could use a lesson in
ating effectively, working more efficiently, and navigating uncertainty.'
Perri, CEO, ProdUX Labs

a new way of working–quickly and simply.'
el Barritt, Managing Director, Sullivan Cuff Software Ltd

Being Agile in Business

PEARSON

At Pearson, we believe in learning – all kinds of learning for all kinds of people. Whether it's at home, in the classroom or in the workplace, learning is the key to improving our life chances.

That's why we're working with leading authors to bring you the latest thinking and best practices, so you can get better at the things that are important to you. You can learn on the page or on the move, and with content that's always crafted to help you understand quickly and apply what you've learned.

If you want to upgrade your personal skills or accelerate your career, become a more effective leader or more powerful communicator, discover new opportunities or simply find more inspiration, we can help you make progress in your work and life.

Pearson is the world's leading learning company. Our portfolio includes the Financial Times and our education business, Pearson International.

Every day our work helps learning flourish, and wherever learning flourishes, so do people.

To learn more, please visit us at **www.pearson.com/uk**

Being Agile in Business

Discover faster smarter, leaner ways to work

Belinda Waldock

PEARSON

Harlow, England • London • New York • Boston • San Francisco • Toronto • Sydney
Auckland • Singapore • Hong Kong • Tokyo • Seoul • Taipei • New Delhi
Cape Town • São Paulo • Mexico City • Madrid • Amsterdam • Munich • Paris • Milan

Pearson Education Limited
Edinburgh Gate
Harlow CM20 2JE
United Kingdom
Tel: +44 (0)1279 623623
Web: www.pearson.com/uk

First published 2015 (print and electronic)

© Belinda Waldock 2015 (print and electronic)

The right of Belinda Waldock to be identified as author of this work has been asserted by her in accordance with the Copyright, Designs and Patents Act 1988.

Pearson Education is not responsible for the content of third-party internet sites.

ISBN: 978-1-292-08370-4 (print)
          978-1-292-08372-8 (PDF)
          978-1-292-08371-1 (eText)
          978-1-292-08373-5 (ePub)

British Library Cataloguing-in-Publication Data
A catalogue record for the print edition is available from the British Library

Library of Congress Cataloging-in-Publication Data
A catalog record for the print edition is available from the Library of Congress

10 9 8 7 6 5 4 3 2 1
19 18 17 16 15

Text design by Design Deluxe
Cover design by Two Associates

Print edition typeset in Mundo Sans 9.5/13pt by 71
Printed by Ashford Colour Press Ltd, Gosport

NOTE THAT ANY PAGE CROSS REFERENCES REFER TO THE PRINT EDITION

CONTENTS

ABOUT THE AUTHOR

Belinda Waldock is an agile business coach and a professionally qualified Institute of Leadership and Management (ILM) coach and mentor in business management with a Computer Science degree. Over the past 15 years Belinda has worked with small to medium-sized businesses in the UK, supporting information and communication technology (ICT) adoption and, more recently, agile adoption through Oxford Innovation. As programme manager and business coach for Agile Innovation, Belinda has worked with a broad range of high-growth businesses across most business sectors to adopt agile practices to leverage their growth aspirations.

Belinda works independently as an agile business coach, facilitator and trainer and supports a wide array of businesses, teams and individuals to adopt agile. She is part of the organising committee for one of the world's leading agile conferences, 'Agile on the Beach', held each September in Falmouth, Cornwall. Belinda has helped to develop and grow the conference over the past four years and is a regular speaker, sharing her experiences of adopting and using agile beyond the software sector. She also supports Software Cornwall, a small, high-growth cluster network of software development companies, and is a business advisor for Young Enterprise.

THE BUSINESS AND PERSONAL PERSPECTIVE

There are very few people in the world of business coaching who can take a complex situation or challenge and turn it into a simple series of options or solutions. Belinda manages exactly this by working agile. Many of the big names in the agile story are better marketers than real agents of change. Belinda is different, in many ways. She has a truly original message and a wonderfully light-hearted style of delivery, in her book and in her workshops. The way she guides people through what they see as a maze, to that 'wow!' moment of clarity, is fun to observe. This is partly a product of her high level of skill and practice, while also an indication of who she really is as a person.

I first met Belinda some years ago when we started working as part of a team of business coaches and mentors for high-growth start-up and small and medium-sized enterprises (SME). We were coaching business entrepreneurs and established organisations' directors and their senior teams on a one-to-one basis, or in workshops. A few years ago, Belinda introduced us to the world of agile, until then used almost exclusively in the software industry. By adapting this to regular businesses and using her way of cutting up challenges into bite-sized chunks, and looking at the world of complex project management and flipping it to use 'low tech' sticky notes, she helped directors, managers, entrepreneurs and individuals to find that breakthrough 'Aha!' moment, fast. She opened up a new way of quickly planning, reviewing and changing, short iterations, saving time once wasted in (long . . .) pointless meetings.

In her book, Belinda shows you a fresh new approach; a faster, more visual way of checking, proving and validating all those things that too often we juggle inside our (over) busy head. Using her book to navigate the easy and fun process of getting control of any situation, she guides you through better uses of time, tools and methods. The benefits are quickly measurable by how much you embrace what you read and put into practice, both in your business and personal life. Belinda makes it effortless to get it, from the basics, to the more in-depth cultural changes that many strive to achieve, but few will reach without using Belinda's agile roadmap. A small investment in time and effort to read this book will enable a profound change for the good in how you work in the future.

We all collaborate in one way or another and, again, Belinda shows some winning ways for sharing information, allocating workload fairly and clearly and enabling everyone to feel a valued team player. Belinda has assisted me greatly with my clients and I always look forward to working with her or co-facilitating agile sessions with new or established businesses. I use the whole agile way of working with both business and private clients. No more need for complex, computer-based project management tools, hidden from view and taking hours to recalculate when the inevitable unexpected changes take place, on a regular basis. Now I 'get it out of my head' and, with Belinda's agile visual tools and methods, I look at it from a variety of perspectives and can share or ask for help from whoever is in my virtual team. Learning this is easy, for all ages and experiences.

If you want to save time, that precious commodity, avoid waste, communicate on workload and resources with friends or colleagues, get reading – short bursts and put it into action – the agile way.

Good luck with your book, Belinda, it will help many others as it has helped me and all my clients to date. The future looks much clearer . . . agile.

William T. Cairley, business and personal coach, Master Business Practitioner NLP

THE TECHNICAL AND SOFTWARE PERSPECTIVE

What is agile? Ask 100 agilists and you will probably get 101 answers. I can give you half a dozen definitions myself, but none are comprehensive. And agile is a moving target, too, it changes. In order to answer the question I need to know why you are asking.

For me, the hallmark of agile is learning. Agile organisations are learning organisations. Normally, when one says **organisation** one means **company,** maybe a hospital, maybe a charity, or maybe just a team.

Once upon a time agile was inherently associated with software development. Software development may always be the home of agile, but it no longer defines agile. Agile has slipped the leash, it is out there in the big world. Changing the big world.

Agile was a response to the problems that much information technology (IT) work – particularly bespoke development and internal corporate work – faces. Using such an approach, the originators drew on what was **seen to work** at the successful companies – largely software vendors.

And it is important to emphasise the **seen to work**. Agile, as we know it today, began life in the patterns community. The patterns community values existing knowledge, the capture and sharing of this knowledge. Not **best practice** – that term implies the practice cannot be bettered and someone somewhere has decided what is **best.** Rather, just good practice that is seen to work, repeatedly. Those values have been handed down from the patterns community to the agile community. Those values are embodied in this book.

What Belinda has captured here are practices that have been seen (with her own eyes) to work. Some of these practices are taken directly from the software world, some have been adapted, and some have come from elsewhere. In this book she gives her answer to the question: 'Can agile work outside of software?'

These practices are described not in dry abstract terms but in the places they are seen and used. In the **real world** – in actual businesses, in actual teams, in real, non-software businesses.

At its simplest, agile is about practices. You can pick up this book and adopt a few agile practices. Certainly agile can be seen as a toolkit from which to choose. In doing so, you might make your team better, you may relieve a pain point or two. But will that deliver the state of being agile? No.

To be truly agile requires a state of mind, a mindset that informs every decision. An agile state of being takes more than following a few practices.

As Woody Allen might say, 'Agile without the mindset is an empty experience but, as empty experiences go, you've got to admit, it's one of the best.' A little bit of agile can make you better but, if you embrace agile with your mind as well as your body, it can make you world-class.

Being truly agile is a mindset, a culture and, ultimately, a business strategy. Right now, the best tools known to deliver that state are in the agile toolkit. Why might you want to be agile? Well, that is a question you must answer for yourself.

Finally, Belinda's stories are refreshing because they are from outside software; she works outside of software and she is outside of the usual agile names. In a way, this book could be written only by someone like Belinda, because it needed to be written by someone outside of software, someone who understands IT but does not live IT.

My hope – my mental model of agile adoption, in fact – is not that you read a book and have agile epiphany. But, rather, that you read this book, you try a few things, you find they work, you are enthused to try some more, learn some more. The process repeats: the more you learn, the more you try; the more success you have, the more you do. Of course, you have the odd failure along the way, but the good is enough to keep you trying. The hard bit is not learning to be agile; the hard bit is unlearning old ways that may have brought success in the past.

Learn and be prepared to unlearn and, one day, you will have the agile mindset. Agile is no longer a good, albeit empty experience, it is fulfilling and there can be no going back.

Allan Kelly, author *of Xanpan, Team Centric Agile Software Development; Business Patterns for Software Developers;* **and** *Changing Software Development: Learning to be Agile.*

ACKNOWLEDGEMENTS

There are many people I would like to thank for their part in making this possible.

I would like to thank Mike Barritt, who introduced me to agile, and his son Jim Barritt, who introduced him to agile, and the team at Oxford Innovation. Thank you to Allan Kelly for teaching me the core of agile within software, and to James Lewis from Thoughtworks for his 'Millennium Falcon' introduction to lean. I would like to thank them all for their support to push agile beyond the realms of software.

My thanks extend to all the industry agile experts who have spoken at 'Agile on the Beach' and supported the software sector in Cornwall over the past four years and who have shared their wealth of knowledge and experience of agile and lean. More inclusively, I would like to thank the huge movement of software developers and others involved in the creation and evolution of agile: it is truly open collaboration and innovation that has made this methodology such a powerful and effective tool for business in today's world.

Thanks go to all the businesses that I have had the pleasure of working with in developing agile both within software and beyond software into a variety of sectors, especially Toby Parkins who has been around from the beginning as a client, colleague and friend.

Special thanks to coaches William Cairley and Karon Clark for sharing their wealth of coaching skills and knowledge, and having the faith in me to push the boundaries and step beyond my comfort zone.

Personal thanks to all my friends and colleagues, especially the 'girls' Marie, Teresa, Louise and Vanessa for their late-night book reviews. I feel

ACKNOWLEDGEMENTS

it probably right here that I should also thank my dog Fiddy and the horses for their animal magic. And special thanks to my Nanna Win for being a guiding force and leading light and to Rich, for always being there for me.

And, finally, special thanks to Eloise Cook, business editor at Pearson, for her positivity and support in writing this book and helping me to get my thoughts onto paper and making this book a reality.

For Nanna Win

x

PUBLISHER'S ACKNOWLEDGEMENTS

We are grateful to the following for permission to reproduce copyright material:

Figures

Figure 8.1 from Jonathan Passmore, ed., *Excellence in Coaching – The Industry Guide*, Kogan Page (Alexander, Graham 2006) Republished with permission of Kogan Page. Permission conveyed through Copyright Clearance Center, Inc.; Figure 15.2 from *7 Habits of Highly Effective People*, Simon & Schuster (Covey, Stephen 1989) Reproduced with permission; Figures 18.3 and 18.4 from 'Building the Millennium Falcon : Lean and Lego', Presentation by James Lewis at Agile on the Beach 2011 http://agileonthebeach.com/2011-2/2011-video/ Reproduced with permission; Figure 24.1 from *Diffusion of Innovation*, 5th ed., The Free Press (Rogers, Everett M. 1995) Reprinted with the permission of The Free Press, a Division of Simon & Schuster, Inc. Copyright © 1995, 2003 by Everett M. Rogers. Copyright © 1962, 1971, 1983, by Free Press, a Division of Simon & Schuster, Inc. All rights reserved; Figure 26.1 from *The Emotional Intelligence Quickbook*, Fireside (Bradberry, Travis and Greaves, Jean 2005) Reprinted with the permission of Fireside, a Division of Simon & Schuster, Inc. Copyright © 2003 by Talent Smart. Copyright © 2005 by Travis Bradberry, Ph.D. and Jean Greaves, Ph.D. All rights reserved.

Text

Extract: Agile software development; definition retrieved from Wikipedia (2014) http://en.wikipedia.org/wiki/Agile_software_development, Text is

PUBLISHER'S ACKNOWLEDGEMENTS

available under the Creative Commons Attribution-ShareAlike License, http://creativecommons.org/licenses/by-sa/3.0/; Extract: from Active Listening; definition retrieved from Wikipedia (2014) http://en.wikipedia.org/wiki/Active_listening, Text is available under the Creative Commons Attribution-ShareAlike License, http://creativecommons.org/licenses/by-sa/3.0/; Extract: adapted from Agile Manifesto and Principles behind the Agile Manifesto, http://agilemanifesto.org/, Kent Beck, Mike Beedle, Arie van Bennekum, Alistair Cockburn, Ward Cunningham, Martin Fowler, James Grenning, Jim Highsmith, Andrew Hunt, Ron Jeffries, Jon Kern, Brian Marick, Robert C. Martin, Steve Mellor, Ken Schwaber, Jeff Sutherland and Dave Thomas. © 2001, the above authors: this declaration may be freely copied in any form, but only in its entirety through this notice; Extract from Systems Thinking; definition retrieved from Wikipedia (2014) http://en.wikipedia.org/wiki/Systems_thinking, Text is available under the Creative Commons Attribution-ShareAlike License, http://creativecommons.org/licenses/by-sa/3.0/; Extract from Building the Millennium Falcon : Lean and Lego; presentation by James Lewis at Agile on the Beach 2011 http://agileonthebeach.com/2011-2/2011-video/ reproduced with permission.

In some instances we have been unable to trace the owners of copyright material, and we would appreciate any information that would enable us to do so.

INTRODUCTION

Welcome. This book provides business professionals with a philosophy, strategy and suite of tools to help you work smarter, leaner and succeed faster. It will help you to:

- understand and apply agile methods in your working world;

- discover strategies and tools to make you work faster and better;

- find out how to anticipate change and navigate uncertainty;

- gain immediate clarity and control in any situation;

- streamline and improve your day-to-day workflow;

- uncover new ways to communicate and collaborate.

Adopting agile and lean methodologies can help to bring success faster by structuring your time differently. For example, if you find yourself in long planning meetings where you feel your time would be better spent doing some work, agile and lean provides a model for quick meetings with clear actions on what to do next.

It will provide you with tools to simplify communication and visibility in your working environment, ensuring the best use of time and resources. Use the tools with your colleagues to improve your abilities as a team player.

Use this book to find ways to identify strengths and opportunities, and uncover barriers and bottlenecks that are limiting your performance. This simple method and toolbox enables you to turn ideas into reality, using an approach that embraces learning and collaboration. As well as tactics, tools, templates, materials and guides, this book contains case studies and exercises to find the best way for you to thrive and succeed in any situation.

I assume you have picked this book primarily because you would like to become better at what you do. You want to make your job easier, increase enjoyment and satisfaction and generate positive results so that you can progress and excel in your career.

You may have a great opportunity on the horizon that you wish to explore, or you may feel stuck in your current position. You may be firefighting in your job day to day, going through extreme change, whether personally or as an organisation, which means the future is uncertain and decisions have to be made. You may be simply intrigued by a new technique for becoming a better business professional.

Whether your personal preference is to take a scientific or a creative approach to your work, these methods have been found to enable both approaches to be incorporated. The tools and methods are structured to allow you to pick out the bits that work for you. The case studies, shown by ⬢, and exercises, shown by ◢ , will help you to adapt and evolve them to suit your style and environment.

The book is split into sections to help you to approach and practise being more agile in your working environment.

The approach in this book is an adaptation of ideas and concepts from agile and lean, taking the best of both to present one unified way of working. The practical heart of the book is Part 3, where you yourself can experiment by personally adopting agile tactics and tools. The book is divided into four parts:

- **Part 1 Being agile** – defines what agile is, the characteristics of an agile and lean business professional and the reasoning for developing these traits within your working practices.

- **Part 2 Agile thinking** – explores why we want and need to be agile in the jobs we do, and the drivers and beliefs needed to adopt an agile approach.

- **Part 3 Agile approaches** – the methods, techniques, tools, materials, practices that give you the structure to be able to act in an agile way.

- **Part 4 Agile culture** – will help you to consider how you can scale and share agile with those you work with, simple steps on how to create a great working environment through collaboration, and how to expand your agility beyond yourself to your teams and organisation.

These techniques can be used to help you beyond your professional life too, whether it is a project to renovate your house, or just thinking through something that is playing on your mind to gain some perspective and find a way forward.

Discover how to anticipate change and navigate uncertainty.

Gain immediate clarity and control in any situation.

Streamline and improve your day-to-day workflow.

Uncover new ways to communicate and collaborate.

Part 1

Being agile

1. Agile background

> **KEY LEARNING POINT**
>
> Learn about the sources of the methods and practices behind agile.

Agile is a globally recognised term for a set of methods and practices that have emerged in the technology sectors to improve the development of software (first named as a software development methodology in 2001 in the 'Manifesto for Agile Software Development', http://agilemanifesto.org). Agile draws upon other management methods such as lean, *kanban* and coaching. Agile has evolved within the software sector to support project management, time management, quality improvement and team performance. The agile methodology provides a change and decision support structure and toolkit.

> **'Agile software development is a group of software development methods in which requirements and solutions evolve through collaboration between self-organizing, cross-functional teams. It promotes adaptive planning, evolutionary development, early delivery, continuous improvement and encourages rapid and flexible response to change. '**
>
> **AGILE SOFTWARE DEVELOPMENT – WIKIPEDIA, 2014 (available under the Creative Commons Attribution ShareAlike License)**

Lean is a methodology that was developed within the manufacturing sector (derived from the Toyota Production System in the 1990s) to support mass production with an ability to continuously improve both the products and manufacturing processes. Lean emphasises a model that looks to take out cost and add value in a business's core activities. Agile draws on the objectives of reducing waste and that of promoting and prioritising activities that add value.

Kanban is a Japanese word meaning signboard. Within agile is it used as a visual representation of work in progress. The method was developed as a system by Taiichi Ohno, Toyota's chief engineer, to maintain a high level of production as well as to manage continuous improvement of products. Kanban is demand-driven in that work is produced on demand, based on customer behaviour and, where possible, just in time. Improvements are responded to quickly when demand for change is observed and integrated into production and delivery processes. The use of kanban within software development has been developed since as a visual tool to help manage the delivery of software solutions (by David J. Anderson, see Wikipedia: http://en.wikipedia.org/wiki/Kanban_%28development%29) and, more broadly, particularly in the knowledge sector.

Coaching as a process is a person-centred methodology, which promotes a solution-focused, goal-orientated approach to personal and professional development. The method works to enable an individual to achieve a greater state of self-awareness and of the environment and people around them. Agile coaching aims to empower the individual or team to become self-managing and self-organising in reaching their goals.

According to the Massachusetts Institute of Technology MIT, research into the use of agile practices within a business suggests that high-agility businesses generate 30 per cent more profit and grow 37 per cent faster than companies with low agility (Project Management Institute, 2012), see Figure 2.1. Others are beginning to recognise that management methods being used in the technology sectors, particularly in the software sector, are 20 years ahead of traditional management techniques: legacies from the 1980s and 1990s that continue to be used despite significant changes to the business environment since.

Traditional management tactics are unable to cope with the rapid change needed to keep pace with global markets and emerging technologies. Plans are often out of date before they are completed and, by the time a product reaches the market, the consumer has moved onto the next new innovation.

Agile provides a new approach to delivering success in today's working environments, addressing growing issues. Agile is agile in its own right and is evolving and flexing continually to meet changing needs and improve its performance as a management tool.

This book aims to introduce the necessary and essential agile concepts and approaches to help you to begin your agile journey.

2. Agile benefits

> **KEY LEARNING POINT**
>
> Explore the problems that agile can help to solve and the benefits that agile working can bring.

The benefits of being agile include:

- lightening your mental load;
- embracing and managing change;
- delivering value early;
- gaining a competitive edge;
- communicating effectively;
- maintaining workflow and focus;
- making good decisions rapidly;
- enabling personal growth and skills.

Problems to solve

If you can identify with any of these problems, then agile tools and thinking can help you to find a way through to a solution:

- lack of visibility and clarity;
- delays due to blocks and bottlenecks;
- too much work or nothing to do;
- moving goalposts and scope creep;
- uncertainty of a way forward;
- starting projects but not finishing them;
- running late and over budget;
- poor communication/collaborative working;
- managing a changing environment;
- procrastination and low morale.

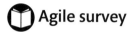 Agile survey

Since 2011 I have been working with small and medium-sized businesses to adopt agile and lean practices into their business strategies and product development practices. These businesses were surveyed to identify the benefits of their adoption of agile.

The survey confirmed the benefits of adoption with agile businesses, reporting:

- a more flexible approach to business;
- improved responsiveness through improved workflow;
- improved communications and team cohesion;
- improved efficiency in general;
- better customer service and satisfaction;
- improved times to market;
- better product testing.

All participants reported enthusiastically from their experiences of implementing agile. Highlights of what was considered to work especially well included testing, process simplification and the board.

Companies also reported better team morale, better time efficiency due to the time management tool and an improved responsiveness to 'mission creep' (Oxford Innovation Services Ltd, 2012).

The survey also identified improved quality, focus and change management through the adoption of agile methods. Many of the businesses reported agile moving into other areas of the business beyond product development, such as strategy, human resources (HR), marketing and sales.

The project was extended in 2012 to work with businesses from a diverse variety of sectors to support the evolvement of agile practices for their use. Following the success of their adoption, the methods have continued to adapt and evolve to be suitable for most business professionals.

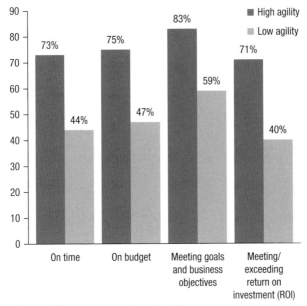

Project success metrics by level of agility

Figure 2.1   Organisational agility
Source: Project Management Institute (2012)

Agile is a flexible working structure that enables you to visualise your workflow in real time to improve:

- responsiveness;
- communications;
- productivity;
- motivation;
- resource management;
- quality of work;
- planning and prioritisation;
- focus.

'"Agile on the Beach 2014" asked conference attendees if being agile made them happy. 95 per cent said yes!'

'AGILE ON THE BEACH 2014' CONFERENCE SURVEY RESULTS

3. Agile characteristics

> **KEY LEARNING POINT**
>
> Identify what being agile means to you.

What does being agile mean to you?

A word or two may spring to mind, or perhaps you picture an agile person, thing or situation. A gymnast, a rock climber, a race horse, a racing yacht, lifeboats, operating theatres, the All Blacks rugby team and a Formula 1 pit stop team are all examples of being agile.

Agile can be defined in a number of ways depending on the context in which they are used to describe someone or something that is responsive, flexible and fast. There are equally numerous ways in which you can apply and adopt agile and lean behaviour.

One simple and easily sourced key tool you need when initially adopting the agile methodology is sticky notes.

The great thing about sticky notes is that they are in themselves very agile.

By their nature sticky notes are flexible and easy to use, you can quickly capture and share information. If you record things on sticky notes they are wonderfully visible and tactile, groups of notes can be easily reviewed and moved around to reorder and restructure them without having to rewrite everything.

Sticky notes aren't permanent or fixed either so you can easily change, swap, add and remove individual notes without impacting other notes.

Sticky notes

The first agile tool is a very simple one: sticky notes (eg Post-it notes or other similar self adhesive notes) are often used for reminders and messages in the office and at home.

Sticky notes are a great tool for adopting an agile approach to get information out of your head and the heads of your colleagues. Use them for ideas, thoughts and expectations, and to break things down into manageable chunks of work that can be reviewed.

Personally, I used to be a real list person, except often it would get to the point where I was so busy or so much was happening that I would spend an inefficient amount of time writing, rewriting and reordering lists. Since adopting sticky notes, the only lists I write these days are shopping lists and, admittedly, even those are always written on a sticky note, as I use agile within my personal and professional life! So, if your list often gets too long, I wholeheartedly recommend buying yourself some sticky notes and giving the method a try.

When mapping out the notes, just let your thoughts flow onto the notes in whatever order they come to mind. The first step is to get your thoughts out of your head and onto paper. They may be linked to a particular topic or goal and, at this point, the notes do not have to be in any particular order or size; the emphasis is on getting things out of your head, and it seems that, in most cases, our minds seem to hold things randomly and not in any particular order.

Each thought should have its own sticky note. If you find yourself writing lists or multiple items on the note, separate these into individual notes. Once you feel you have everything out of your head, then you can begin to order and group your sticky notes into a structure or format that helps you to organise and map these into something that makes sense. The exercises and tools provided in this book provide a number of options for mapping a volume of notes into structures and formats that allow them to be qualified, validated and actioned.

 **Defining agile**

What characteristics do you associate with being agile?

Using your sticky notes, or the following blank diagram, start capturing any words or images that you associate with the word agile.

- Start with a sticky note and write the word agile in the centre.

- Whatever comes to mind, capture these in single words, images or short phrases and write them on more notes, one per note, and place them around your central note, building up a map of associations.

Allow your mind to freely connect to another thought and capture these, too, on separate notes. These could lead you to specific situations relevant to you. Capture occasions where you feel you were agile or lean in your actions or approach, and identify the feelings, values and behaviour in that scenario.

Once that thought is captured on paper, return to thinking of the word 'agile' and see what else comes to mind.

Try not to pause, hesitate or dismiss any thoughts, just write them down as they come to you, one per sticky note; you can always discard them later if you wish. If you do not have any sticky notes yet, use the blank diagram below to capture your thoughts.

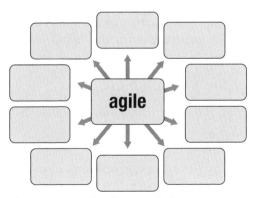

Figure 3.1   Agile characteristics map

The map you create is unlikely to be the same as another, although it may have some commonalities.

Once you have captured your thoughts, study your notes and see if there are connections or themes among them. Look for patterns and relationships and move them around to reflect this. Group similar words together to form key themes.

The meaning of words is unique for every one of us. While there are commonalities, we all perceive and process things slightly differently to the next person. This is a good thing because once we know what we believe to be the definition of something, we can share this with others to ensure there is clarity between ourselves.

The next maps of agile definitions have been created from a number of sources, including group discussions and definitions found online (Figure 3.2). Some almost everyone will say, others are one-offs, and there most certainly are others that are not included here. Figure 3.3 shows key themes, chunking them into seven key agile characteristics.

Using sticky notes with your team, your manager and your customers can be incredibly valuable in ensuring understanding between all parties. The activity of mapping ideas and discussing them supports communication. Communication is a two-way activity: we talk and we listen. To improve your listening skills, active listening is a great technique for helping to ensure you are listening and clarifying what others are telling you.

Mapping definitions

A successful restaurant owner, Andrew, had plans to open a new restaurant. His current restaurant was based in a seaside town and the new restaurant was linked to a local city farm development. His finance manager, Teresa, enthusiastically had taken a lead on producing the initial business plan, and there was informal involvement from his existing marketing manager and non-executive directors.

There were a number of different options for the style, market and product that would model the businesses vision. One particular idea from Andrew was for a diner-style restaurant which, in Teresa's mind, conjured up ideas of a motorway service cafe.

Equipped with the sticky note mapping method and sticky notes, Teresa was armed with a collaboration game to help the team come to a shared vision

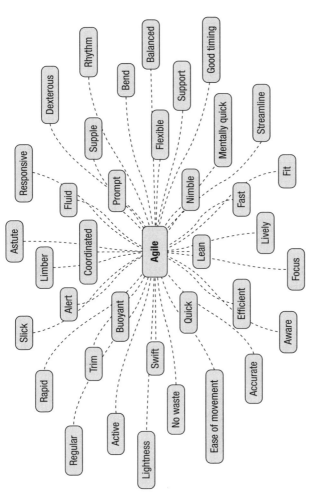

Figure 3.2   Example of an agile characteristics map

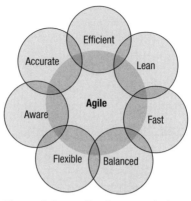

Figure 3.3　Agile characteristics

where an appropriate style, market and product were identified to take forward, or at least differentiate, the number of options that had been suggested.

As they began to explore each idea further, Teresa facilitated this using active listening and clarifying questions such as: 'Can you tell me a little more about this one?' To her relief, when the CEO started to talk about a diner, it became very clear that he was imagining a French bistro, following a recent holiday, fine dining and wonderful surroundings.

After a short time, the team had a number of solid ideas that would work together and that they could explore further. Throughout the conversation, queries were raised and actions set to research and develop each idea further.

The simple activity of mapping out the ideas and discussing them provided a visual aid to promote communication and develop a shared language within the team, so that everyone had a shared understanding of the definition of the goal.

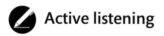 ## Active listening

> 'Active listening is a communication technique used in counselling, training and conflict resolution, which requires the listener to feed back what they hear to the speaker . . . to confirm what they have heard and moreover, to confirm the understanding of both parties.'
>
> WIKIPEDIA – 'ACTIVE LISTENING', 2014. (Available under the Creative Commons Attribution ShareAlike License.)

It is good to ask open questions that help to clarify and understand the topic being discussed:

- What is the goal?
- What do you want?
- What do you not want?
- How would you describe the current situation?
- What is currently stopping you?
- What would work for you?
- What benefits would you like to see?
- What problems need to be solved?
- What would success look like?
- What other options are there?
- Is there anything else?
- Can you tell me more about that?

Use sticky notes to explore your thoughts and perspective.

Key characteristics of agile are:

- **accurate;**
- **efficient;**
- **lean;**
- **flexible;**
- **aware;**
- **fast;**
- **balanced.**

4. Agile logic

KEY LEARNING POINT

Understand the logic behind agile thinking.

> 'According to Darwin's *Origin of Species*, it is not the most intellectual of the species that survives; it is not the strongest that survives; but the species that survives is the one that is able best to adapt and adjust to the changing environment in which it finds itself.'
>
> MEGGINSON (1963)

Thriving during change and uncertainty

In a constantly evolving world that today moves at speed on a global scale, to be successful we must embrace change and not endeavour to resist it.

It would be easier if life were as simple as 'A to B', that everything was mapped out, constant and routine, but it is not. Most things in life have a natural life cycle, which has its own ebb and flow.

Things tend to have their own natural life cycle of usefulness; they are started, grow, mature and then decline. If this life cycle remains unchanged, it will become out of date and inefficient or ineffective. We need to improve and develop our work continuously to disrupt the natural life cycle before it enters decline and causes disruption itself.

Change is the only constant in life.

Working in today's business environment, we all are subject to coping with change. Agile is a method that works when a situation is subject to extreme and constant change and innovation.

When we need to move forward, despite not having answers, this requires us to embrace uncertainty and make decisions based on limited knowledge. We may be operating largely on assumptions and gut feeling. Managers, customers and suppliers change their minds, as do we all, throwing in new ideas, adding to the scope of what they want, yet traditional methods still maintain a need for a fixed specification upfront, a deadline with a set amount of resource and budget, and there is no scope for change.

In order to reach a goal effectively, we must do three things:

1. **Embrace change** Accept change as a reality and accept that goals will change and evolve over time. In order to succeed in times of change, we need to recognise the problems and act appropriately to identify positive ways to mitigate the issues and find solutions before they become a major problem.

2. **Build in learning** In order to ensure we act effectively, we need to give ourselves time to learn and ensure we have the right skills, tools and metrics, so we are aware of the impact of change and our choices to address it.

3. **Expect rework** We do not generally succeed the first time we try something new; we should expect to test and trial our ideas before we find a way that works to deliver value in an efficient and effective way. We accept that in order to reach a goal, we will learn and change our mind in the route to finding a solution to our problem.

There are numerous ways to get to where you want to be, and agile allows you to explore these options, change your mind and improve your solution. It provides a roadmap to find the best path to reaching your goal, whatever that might be.

In software development, a common term used for change and additions to the requirements of software is **scope creep.** As systems get bigger and bigger, engineers need methods that can manage the development of large complex systems that are subject to ongoing changes to their requirements. Agile has developed out of a demand for control in an ever-changing environment.

In business and, more generally, the world in which we live, we are in a constant state of scope creep, with ever-moving goal posts, curve balls that can change the direction we have to take, and revolutions that require us to rethink our tactics completely.

Understanding the journey of change

Change can be difficult and so often we default to try and reject it, preferring the comfort of the familiar and well known. Becoming aware of this instinct to reject change and putting in an effective management structure for handling it can help us to accept and take advantage of change

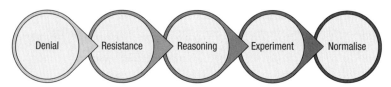

Figure 4.1   Change journey

rather than reject it. Agile provides a structure to move forward quickly and rationally during times of change and uncertainty.

There are numerous models for how we respond naturally to change. All these follow a similar cycle of resistance through to acceptance (see Figure 4.1).

- **Denial** – first off, we are surprised by the change. It caught us unaware and we are in a state of shock; we are stunned and sometimes stalled by it, frozen and unable to react or respond. We question whether the change is real; we deny, ignore and avoid it, pretending it is not happening and carry on as usual.

- **Resistance** – when we accept that the change has happened, we can become frustrated that things have altered and we actively resist the change.

- **Reasoning** – once we realise the change is not going away, and time passes, the emotional driver to resist diminishes: we begin to analyse the situation more rationally and gain a clearer perspective on the actual impact of the change.

- **Experiment** – once accepted, we begin to experiment with adapting to the change, and act to lessen the impact and potentially use it to our advantage to see the opportunities resulting from the change.

- **Normalisation** – as time passes, this change becomes normality and becomes comfortable and expected, with business as usual. The disruption caused by the change becomes a thing of the past and we continue our journey, until the next change interrupts the status quo and the cycle of change begins again.

Awareness of change

Better awareness of how we manage change naturally helps to gain perspective early to respond appropriately and identify opportunities, rather than continued resistance.

Feeling pressured, stressed, stuck and frustrated can be signals of change that have been missed or ignored rather than dealt with. If you have errors creeping into your work, it could be time for a change.

By developing our ability to be aware of change and understand our and others' behaviours and drivers, we are in a better position to handle that change more effectively. Being aware of the process of change can help us to confront it, reason with it and proactively work to integrate that change the best we can.

Agile is a visual method that helps by presenting us with warning signals. It helps to maintain a broader perspective and sight of activities and progress. Visualising our work helps us to see trends, patterns and themes. Being aware of the rhythm of our work enables us to see change early and even predict change and embrace it before it becomes difficult to manage.

> **'There is chaos under the heavens and the situation is excellent.'**
>
> **CHINESE PROVERB**

Read this quote again and take a minute to think about what it is saying. Suggesting that when times are chaotic (which is often a result of change), this is an opportunity for learning and growth. It infers, optimistically, that the situation is good because there is the chance that that change could lead to improvements, new opportunities and benefits.

Change can be incredibly positive, if harnessed and opportunities are identified, and weaknesses are addressed quickly in a responsive rather than a reactive way. If we are reacting to change as it happens, the urgency at this stage provokes a knee-jerk reaction that may not be thought through, it may address only the issue in hand and not see the root of the problem.

The agile method acknowledges that there will be change and so builds in continuous reflection that ensures a structured, considered and timely response. Rather than hope it all works out as planned, we accept change and adopt tactics to manage that change.

Letting go

Letting go of existing processes and systems to adopt agile can be difficult, especially for those who are comfortable with routine. Even if that routine is difficult, it can be hard to acknowledge. There is a need to let go of the existing rules, identify the problem within the process or the system and go through the pain of change in order to achieve a better outcome. Trusting that what is, in effect, a very simple management system like agile to expose and address current problems in your working practices, can be counter-intuitive to some and can take time to accept.

Often, where agile has been adopted, there will be those who are early adopters and those who are slow adopters that lag behind, or may never change. The natural adoption life cycle is aided by the visual and collaborative nature of the method, which works by being inclusive and attractive to those who come into contact with it. It is important to recognise that some are more able to change than others and that while adoption can be encouraged, it cannot be forced.

Adapt and adjust quickly to respond to change and uncertainty:

- **Embrace change**

- **Build in learning**

- **Expect rework**

Part 2

Agile thinking

5. Agile state

> **KEY LEARNING POINT**
>
> Identify the three layers of agility needed to create an agile mindset.

Creating the right state of mind to achieve agility is vital: agile works with change, it sees it as an everyday occurrence and gives us a way of thinking and a structure to map out and manage change by embracing uncertainty through learning and experimentation.

In order to do things well, we must have a **good state of mind, good structure** and **good content.** Agile tools and techniques provide a structure and make it possible to sustain a state of agility (see Figure 5.1).

William T. Cairley, business and personal coach (Master Business Practitioner, Neurolinguistic Programming (NLP)), first introduced me to the three layers of state, structure and content as a coaching tool, especially when presenting.

- **Agile state**

An agile state is achieved by adopting an agile philosophy: the approach, values and beliefs that drive agile behaviour explored in Part 1.

- **Agile structure**

The agile methodology provides structure that supports agile behaviour. The methodology provides the tactics, tools and techniques for managing and thriving during change and embracing uncertainty.

- **Agile content**

The activities, value and resources that deliver the desired solution to meet goals and achieve success.

 **Presenting**

Let's use presenting as an example of how to apply and think about content, structure and state. If delivering a presentation, it is vital that the presenter is focused and in the right frame of mind to allow them to convey

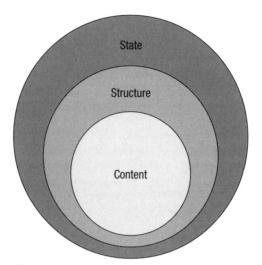

Figure 5.1   Agile state, structure and content

their content in the best way: their tone, mood, pitch and body language must be positive and engaging, if anyone is going to listen to what they have to say.

The presentation must also be structured well so that it flows and makes sense to the listener. The structure will also include details of the presentation, such as timing, audience, branding/layout and style, housekeeping and other relevant elements that guide the structure and format of the presentation.

If the presenter has a good state of mind and a good structure, this should guide and prompt the content of the presentation and help ensure that it is delivered successfully.

6. Agile beliefs

> **KEY LEARNING POINT**
>
> Understand the values and principles behind an agile way of thinking.

Agile in software has a manifesto, a set of beliefs and values that are dedicated to helping to understand the balance needed to ensure success in a changing environment (Agile Manifesto, 2001).

| **'Value *individuals and interactions* over processes and tools.'**

People and their roles and activities should be supported by systems and procedures, not controlled by them. Processes and tools should evoke the best solution rather than limit outcomes and suppress opportunities for continuous improvement.

| **'Value *working solutions* over comprehensive documentation.'**

It is better to have a solution that works than one that meets the specification. With standards trying to pin everything down to the nth degree to ensure consistency and transparency, change can be difficult to embrace if you have to stick to the rules. It is better to have something that works and, by having flexible business management systems, we can adapt more easily to suit each unique environment: it can allow us to personalise and customise solutions.

| **'Value *customer collaboration* over contract negotiation.'**

Forging relationships and building rapport and trust with clients makes it easier to form agreements and deliver value to both parties. If we have a good working relationship with someone, it is far easier to come to a mutual understanding with them. Even if we do not necessarily agree with them, it is easier to compromise because you trust that the person has good reason for the position they take. 'People buy from people' is a common phrase in the sales world: if someone has confidence and trust in you, they are more likely to buy from you. By building relationships with others often we can negotiate ad hoc arrangements, special compensations and flexible working agreements.

| 'Value *responding to change* over following a plan.'

It is important that we map and plan things, but it is true that 'the best-laid plans go to waste' because things change and, if we spend too long planning, we will be acting perpetually late. We need to balance reacting immediately with appropriate planning. To respond to change, we need to understand and learn about the situation, decide on a way forward and act, and repeatedly reflect on progress in order to learn more and adapt our actions accordingly as we go along.

In some instances we can find that over time, interactions, solutions, collaboration and change management are lost to overemphasis on processes, tools, documentation, contracts and plans:

- Personal interaction with people is lost to automated tools and fixed processes.

- Solutions do not work but are well documented and meet all standards.

- Contracts have been secured but collaboration is poor and the relationship breaks down.

- There is no response to change, the initial plan is delivered as originally specified but it is out of date and the customer is not satisfied.

This can happen often when activities have existed and been repeated for a long time and, more broadly, in maturing companies, making them rigid by controlling processes and rules, inhibiting their ability to innovate and change quickly.

Principles behind the Agile Manifesto

The following is a useful list of principles adapted from the Manifesto for Agile Software Development website (Agile Manifesto, 2001):

- The highest priority is to satisfy the customer through early and continuous delivery of valuable working solutions.

- Welcome changing requirements, even late in development. Agile processes harness change for the customer's competitive advantage.

- Deliver working solutions frequently, from a couple of weeks to a couple of months, with a preference for the shorter timescale.

- Business people and developers must work together daily throughout the project.

- Build projects around motivated individuals. Give them the environment and support they need, and trust them to get the job done.

- The most efficient and effective method of conveying information to and within a development team is face-to-face conversation.

- Working solutions are the primary measure of progress.

- Agile processes promote sustainable development. The sponsors, developers and users should be able to maintain a constant pace indefinitely.

- Continuous attention to technical excellence and good design enhances agility.

- Simplicity – the art of maximising the amount of work not done – is essential.

- The best architectures, requirements and designs emerge from self-organising teams.

- At regular intervals, the team reflects on how to become more effective, then tunes and adjusts its behaviour accordingly.

Source: Agile Manifesto and Principles (c) 2001, authors: this declaration may be freely copied in any form, but only in its entirety through this notice.

While procedure, documentation, contracts and plans are important, an agile professional gives priority to:

- people;

- working solutions;

- collaboration;

- change.

7. Agile method

KEY LEARNING POINT

Discover how to adopt a learning-driven approach that delivers results early and allows for improvement.

Agile is a learning-based methodology and a routine of small incremental improvements with time to repeat, reflect and learn regularly recommended. It is an approach that trusts we learn from experience, and we need to provide ways to identify and embed this learning.

When we want to get something done, generally we decide on our goal, define exactly what we want to do, develop that and then deliver it. We try to do this often as a linear process, deciding everything upfront before we design and build, achieving something as good as possible before releasing it.

In software this is known as the **waterfall** model, first described in 1970 by Winston W. Royce (see Figure 7.1). When carrying out small and well-defined projects, one visit to each stage in a linear flow is sufficient.

If there is an element of unknown and the solution required is perhaps uncertain, large or complex, then one pass simply is not enough to reach a satisfactory result. Additionally, this model provides no scope to engage with the client other than at the start and end of the process.

The reality is that change happens during development and requirements may have to be rethought and revisited, but the waterfall method does

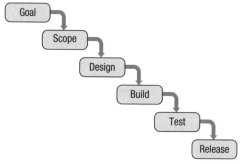

Figure 7.1   Waterfall model

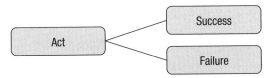

Figure 7.2 Success/failure optimism

not account for rework. This can lead to scope creep, when changes must be made, and that can lead to delays and increase in costs and resources.

In order to create an agile state of mind, we need to approach problems with the recognition that it may take more than one attempt to solve the problem, and that the more we know about the problem, the greater equipped we are to find an effective and lasting solution.

The optimist in us all likes to believe that we will get it right first time (see Figure 7.2).

Realistically, when we are doing something we have not done before, it will take us a few attempts at least to achieve the result we are seeking. It may be that we have to continue to revise the solution to get the benefits and value we require.

In order to achieve the best performance possible there is a cycle of practice and rehearsal that we must undertake to form the habit and allow ourselves to get used to doing things a particular way.

The more we do something, generally the better we get at it; we are able to automate ourselves and even carry out tasks without any conscious effort, such as driving a car or riding a bike. It becomes second nature and easy to replicate without much conscious effort.

Interestingly, though, often the reason activities become ineffective or stuck over time is because we have become too habitual and not stopped to review and change our ways in order to maintain performance.

Each time we repeat the action we refine and hone it and get closer to success until, finally, we reach a point where we are satisfied with the result. In this sense, it is not really failing if the result gets us closer to success and we continue to experiment until we reach a satisfactory outcome.

There is no such thing as failure if we choose to learn from it in order to be successful at a later date. The journey to success can feel like a game of Snakes and Ladders: there will be shortcuts and setbacks along the way, which we need to identify and respond to, and we cannot predict them all. Agile provides a method to adopt a learning attitude, which allows

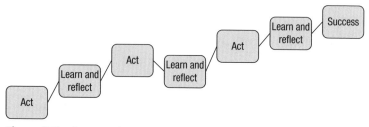

Figure 7.3   Journey to success

us to harness our natural ability to navigate a journey to success through reflection and learning (see Figure 7.3).

Satisfaction does not necessarily mean literal perfection, but it does mean it is good enough to satisfy the requirements. We may need to refine this further, tweak and develop again further along in time, but a good enough solution is often as much as is needed.

Agile takes this journey into account to provide a method that builds in change and makes it easier to work towards a goal in unfamiliar, uncertain and changing situations.

Conservatory drip challenge

A few years ago, around November time, I decided to put a new carpet down in my conservatory ready for hosting a family Christmas. The conservatory had a minor leak that meant a slow drip appeared if there was very heavy rain between where the conservatory joined the main house.

The journey was mapped out: remove the old carpet, remove facia to find out where the leak is, use silicon to seal the leaking area, clean and fit new carpet. With a deadline six weeks away and the scope of work being around two days in total, the job seemed very doable within the constraints given.

The actual journey was really rather different and resulted in the conservatory not being completed until February. There were are number of issues which led me to under estimate the scope of work, due mostly to a lack of skill, knowledge and a number of optimistic assumptions.

When I took up the old carpet, I found the floor was significantly wet and damp and would need to be replaced; when the facia was removed, it was clear the roof had multiple leaks. I was out of my depth as far as my DIY skills were concerned, so I contacted a roofing contractor. The first roofing contractor managed to stop two of the leaks, the second conservatory contractor managed to stop another two, but the final leak in one corner persisted. Each time a leak was fixed, I would have to wait until it rained to see if it was fixed or not.

Eventually, after a lot of watching, thinking and application of silicone in a number of locations, the final leak was stopped, the roof and floor began to dry out and the new floor and carpet could be fitted. The complete elapsed time was three months and the total active time and cost was around five times longer and higher than expected.

The reality is that until you have started a job and investigated the problem properly, any assumptions you make about the size and complexity of the problem and the nature of a satisfactory solution can be wrong. Especially if you have little experience and little understanding of the job.

Traditional practices like the waterfall approach aspire, unrealistically, to achieve a fixed specification from the start and success in one pass with a fixed amount of resources and time. These practices seek to fix and control each component of the solution and limit variance; they do not have the flexibility to change and alter course so, if this occurs, the solution is unable to change to adapt with the evolving environment.

Agile and lean practices work in small incremental improvements, expecting change, building flexible solutions that are continuously managed and resource- and time-committed, based on the value delivered. The more valuable a solution becomes, the more resource and time is assigned to it to build on this success or, alternatively, if the solution is not progressing as desired, resources can be reallocated.

Small incremental improvements

Agile ensures that there is scope to change by not committing everything upfront: agile breaks down the work into deliverable chunks and plans to undertake multiple cycles through the process. Agile aims to deliver early, often and consistently to satisfy changing requirements long term. The first cycle looks to validate needs and deliver something of value early, if possible, against the goal and scope (see Figure 7.4). Rather than including everything from the start and aiming to take the waterfall approach to completion in one linear start-to-finish project, agile accepts that often there is no ultimate finish line or ending, and that work will be added along the way, especially if performance is good and growth in demand for work increases.

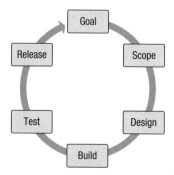

Figure 7.4   Incremental improvement cycle

By working in this way, not all the resources and time are used to get to the first and only solution. Agile allows time and resources to be flexible and incremental, based on early results, leaving capacity to revisit our decisions and designs, build a number of versions and deliver value earlier in the process, which has the benefit of enabling us to gain feedback and learn, to help understand and improve as part of the process.

> **An agile incremental approach allows us to build momentum and traction towards a solution that delivers value early and then continues to improve and scale incrementally.**

So, rather than a linear process, it is an iterative cycle. An iteration is a repeated cycle of recurring improvement where, each time we cycle, small incremental improvements are made. Solutions are formulated, built and tested incrementally, using short cycles of activity that are interwoven with time to think, reflect and learn.

Eat cake!

Projects are like eating a cake! A cake that is made up of layers: at the bottom an integration layer of sponge, then a layer of jam for testing, another sponge representing build, some cream filling for design, another layer of sponge for the scope, and the icing on top is the goal.

Think about how you might eat that cake: you will not eat the cake layer by layer, instead you cut slices from the cake; the cake gets eaten slice by slice rather than layer by layer. Think of your project as a cake and tackle it by eating it in small slices.

Model the solution a little, define the way forward, build and develop a proportion of the solution and then deliver it for feedback before deciding what to do next. Then move through the cycle again, defining activity, doing some work and then delivering this again for review and feedback, and so this continues until we reach a solution that is fit for purpose.

If our goal is not viable in the existing environment, we need to establish this as quickly as possible with the minimum of cost. Agile embraces the reality that we do not have all the answers when we start, and that the best solutions are developed when we can determine our actions in real time as the environment evolves and changes.

Agile thinking knows the reality that a number of versions may need to be created before success is reached, and it is a journey of learning that needs to be navigated and refined to find the best solution. By making changes incrementally rather than in bulk this limits the number of changes that are made at one time, so that the impact of those changes can be measured and controlled.

We need to have a conscious acceptance that making mistakes is ok when we are trying to solve a problem. Understanding that it will take a few attempts to get it right means that we are willing to make mistakes to expand our knowledge and accelerate us towards the answer, or a better solution.

Learn – act – reflect cycle

Agile works in small incremental cycles of action, interleaved with time for reflection and learning (see Figure 7.5). (Based on reflective coaching models and technology start-up models, such as build – measure – learn, as defined by Eric Ries in his book *The Lean Startup, 2011*.) Improvement and change is embedded in day-to-day activity rather than as a separate activity.

Figure 7.5   Learn – Act – Reflect cycle

Learn

- Agree goals and objectives.
- Metrics and measures are established to measure success.
- Map existing reality.
- Establish scope and requirements.
- Estimate activities and rank activities.
- Identify options for next cycle of activity.
- Consider previous action and reflection to establish key learning points.
- Identify future learning needs.
- Decide and plan next activities, based on learning and reflection.

Act

- A period of action and development of a set amount of work.
- Work prioritised by reflection and learning.
- Activity is tracked and measured to provide defined metrics.
- Limited change to scheduled work during current batch of activity.

Reflect

- Test, release and gain feedback from those dependent on activity.
- Review and reflect on last cycle of activity and results.
- Reflect on what has gone well and what can be improved.
- Review progress and outputs through metrics and measures.
- Reflect on overall direction and progress.
- Identify options and ways forward for next cycle of work.

Feedback-driven delivery

A team wanted to improve the service they were delivering to clients and increase customer satisfaction. The business surveyed clients on completion of work to gain feedback on their service and to find out how satisfied the customer was with the work, asking if the customer would recommend them to a friend.

It was felt that the customer experience could be improved further, but how to do this was not clear. The business began to collect feedback early from the customer and, one week into the service, a survey was undertaken. This survey asked the customer how satisfied they were with the initial service; it also asked:

- what the business was doing well;

- what could be better;

- if there were any issues or priorities they would like to flag.

These questions enabled the business to gain early feedback and establish what the priorities of the customer were: for example, a customer may be pleased with progress, but wish to change priorities. Using this individual information, the team were able to feed this back to the delivery team and they could adapt their focus to concentrate on the issues most important to the customer.

The business continued to gather feedback from the client at the end of the service and those that had been asked early for feedback reported a higher level of satisfaction in the service. They appreciated the ongoing engagement and the opportunity to focus on their priorities, making them more likely to recommend a friend to the business.

Gathering feedback early works to improve the customer experience by highlighting areas that can be improved. By acting to improve the customers' experience, this highlighted areas of service and improvements to current systems and processes that also could be used with future customers.

By gathering feedback early from the customer, the business was able to learn and focus its service to better fit the customer and their needs. Rather than surveying at the end, when no changes could be made as you would with the waterfall method, the early information enabled the technicians to act accordingly during the early phases to improve the experience for clients.

- **Learn – continuous learning helps us to understand, gain clarity and continuously improve.**

- **Act – small sprints of action are sustainable and enable us to regularly review and adapt our direction.**

- **Reflect – reviewing and measuring our progress can help us to learn and inform us on the best direction to take.**

8. Agile goals

> **KEY LEARNING POINT**
>
> Learn how to be solution-focused and how to clarify
> what you want to achieve.

A key element of agile is not scoping everything out in detail at the beginning of the process. It takes the approach that we capture and review what we know, establish our goals and vision, our key objectives and then we act in small, incremental improvements based on validating the vision and options going forward.

Things rarely happen in the way we picture they will. We need a method that allows us to embrace the situation as it unfolds and make decisions as necessary to keep us on track towards our goals, and even change our goals, if that is the right thing to do.

By clarifying our goals and objectives we can work towards outcomes and value that we aim to achieve. Agile manages activities based on our performance towards these objectives rather than a pre-planned set of instructions and fixed requirements. The method helps the team to find the best solution rather than define and control it from the start.

To establish our goals, we need to understand and clarify where we are now, where we want to be, and what the options are to get from one to the other.

GROW model

GROW is a coaching tool established in the 1980s by Graham Alexander and Jonathan Passmore (Passmore, 2006) to help identify the goals, reality, options and way forward in any situation and is explained further in this and the next three sections (see Figure 8.1).

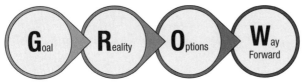

Figure 8.1 GROW model
Source: Passmore (2006)

- **Goal** – what is the goal to be achieved?

- **Reality** – what is the reality of the situation?

- **Option** – what are the options and their impact?

- **Way forward** – what actions will be taken forward?

Use sticky notes to map ideas and map out a GROW model (see Figure 8.2).

Establishing goals

Consider the questions below to help identify goals and objectives:

- What are your goals and aspirations?

- Why is this important?

- What do you want to achieve?

- What are the objectives of that goal?

- What problem needs to be solved?

- What does success look like?

- What results/value/benefits do you want to achieve?

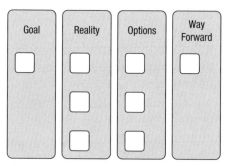

Figure 8.2   GROW model ideas map

✒ Mapping goals

In the next section there will be practical exercises to help you, so consider now:

- What are you going to use agile for? For example, day-to-day workload, delivering a project, new product development, marketing campaign, managing a team.

- What goals are you hoping to achieve by adopting agile?

A simple way to establish goals is to come up with a list of things you want to achieve and how you would like things to be. Adversely, initially, you may find yourself thinking of things you do not want; capture these in the right column and then consider what the alternative want might be.

Map out wants and do not wants using sticky notes (see Figure 8.3).

By having a clear picture of what you want, this should help clarify goals and aspirations. We will use these goals later and use agile to identify the activities you want to change and improve.

By establishing the goals you want to achieve, you can be motivated towards what you want rather than away from what you do not want.

Reality, options and way forward of GROW will be covered in the next three sections.

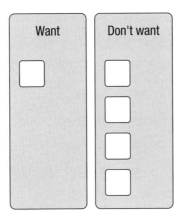

Figure 8.3   Want/don't want map

9. Agile reality

> **KEY LEARNING POINT**
>
> Learn how to take a reality check to help you gain focus and balance.

In order to improve what we do, we need to be aware of what currently happens. The R in GROW is for reality check: to look into goals further and observe the reality of the situation from different points of view in order to uncover the real problem. Analysing where we are now enables us to set a starting point for getting where we want to be. In order to reach a goal, we need to understand the current way of doing things and what the problems are with existing processes and systems, so we can establish the frustrations and friction that those cause.

 ## Open questioning

Open questioning is a tool that can be used to find out more about a current situation or scenario. Open questions are questions that require a fuller answer than just yes/no: a yes/no answer is to a closed question, as there are only limited responses.

For example:

Closed question: Is your cup of tea cold? Yes/no.

Open question: Why is your tea cold? My tea is cold because. . .

Here is a list of open questions:

- **Why** is the work currently undertaken?
- **How** is the work currently undertaken?
- **What** value does this deliver?
- **What** currently works well?
- **What** could be better?
- **Where** are the points of friction – problems, constraints, blocks?
- **What** would happen if you did not achieve your goal?

- What resources are available (time, budget, materials, people, skills, knowledge . . .).

- **What** and **who** is dependent or involved more widely?

- **What** does not get done?

- Are there key dates or milestones that need to be considered?

- **Why**?

 ## Root cause analysis – ask why?

The root cause analysis was first used in the 1950s by NASA. A great way to discover the root cause of a problem is to use the 'five whys', which originates from the Toyota Production System (developed by Sakichi Toyoda). It drills down into an issue to discover the underlying problem or defect simply by asking what the problem is and then continually asking why that is until the root cause of the issue is uncovered. The question simply can be the use of the single word 'why' or woven into the context of the conversation.

Problem statement: My cup of tea is cold and I wanted a hot cup of tea!

Why? Because the kettle did not boil.

Why? Because the kettle has no power.

Why? Because the fuse has blown.

Why? Because electrical surges cause fuses to blow.

Why? Because there is no surge protection.

Action: Install surge protection to prevent further electrical issues from surges.

This system helps us to dig down into the root cause of the problem and look for ways to prevent it happening again (surge protection) rather than just identifying and fixing the apparent cause (blown fuse).

Mapping reality

By analysing how we spend our time and comparing this to how we would like to spend our time, we can see immediately if we are doing what we need to, if we are getting sidetracked or if we are caught up in the day to day.

The 'caught up in the details' situation is a common issue where we get so caught up in the action that we forget to stop and review progress. When we do, we find we have gone off on a tangent, or things have changed and what we were doing previously does not quite fit anymore.

As a business professional, our time is split between tasks we do as part of our core role and with which we are comfortable and familiar – day-to-day activities – and new activities we are developing for the first time. We may be improving processes, growing our role, learning and developing new skills and knowledge, evolving and changing the way we work.

Depending on your specific role, this may be 70 per cent business as usual doing the day-to-day workload and 30 per cent breaking new ground where we are improving our working environment, laying seeds for ideas, or those wonderful events that come from nowhere and send you rocketing into the unknown. These often come with the promise of wonderful rewards and benefits, and sometimes they do, but sometimes they fade away as quickly as they appeared.

Using the agile dashboard in Section 17, Part 3, current processes and activities can be tracked, which will provide key insights into how the current situation operates. Agile tracking methods help to uncover and reveal blocks and barriers, limitations and restrictions, which can help to get a great view of the current reality of the situation.

Gaining balance

Google employees are encouraged to spend 20 per cent of their time working on new projects and improving their performance by researching and developing new ideas.

(Google 2004 Founders' IPO Letter, http://investor.google.com/corporate/2004/ipo-founders-letter.html, although this idea came originally from 3M).

Slack should be created to enable you to improve your day-to-day working practices, and identify, focus and improve upon the value you deliver

Consider if the balance of your work is right. For example, are you a manager who is spending too much time practically doing instead of managing

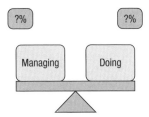

Figure 9.1   Balancing managing and doing

others (see Figure 9.1)? In order to improve, we should focus on where we create the most value. Do you spend enough or too much of your time planning and organising rather than getting on with the job?

Creating slack

A proportion of work is predictable and can be planned for but, if you are growing, then there is always an element of unpredictability to manage.

You may not have any time for breaking new ground, commonly known as **firefighting,** and this leaves little or no time to consolidate learning and ensure work is as efficient and effective as it needs to be. The ideal is to achieve a balance of comfort and consistency with a framework that enables us to review and improve constantly. Analysing the reality can help us to find where the value is generated, while identifying inefficient and non-value-adding activities that may be unnecessary. Agile provides a methodology for visualising the current reality so it can be reviewed and managed continuously.

It is vital to identify how you spend your time, which of your work delivers the most value. How much you can plan, versus how much you need to deal with, as it happens. This helps to maintain an awareness of your work-load and maintain a good balance of planning or responding and doing or improving (see Figure 9.2).

A great agile concept is to ensure you create slack within your time so that you can explore new options and opportunities, gain new skills and make new connections. This time can be spent improving and increasing your performance.

Figure 9.2   Balancing doing and improving

Enabling change

Peter, the founder of a growing surveying company, was finding that as his business and his team grew, it was hard to keep track of everything. The systems used when the team was small were no longer working efficiently: the team was starting lots of change projects to improve systems but they were not being finished. The team seemed to be constantly firefighting the sheer volume of work as well as failing to implement a number of change projects.

The teams within the business took time to map out the current improvement projects that had been started and put these onto a board in the office. Utilising any slack time they had available, after day-to-day activities, project activities were selected that they would have time to action. Any new projects or actions were added and discussed and scheduled in to action. By doing this, the team was able to see and manage the projects they were working on; it also enabled management to capture ideas for improvements and schedule them appropriately, as time was available.

By using agile tactics the teams were able to deliver value early within the projects by developing the elements that delivered the most benefit and value to the team. As these benefits were realised and efficiencies in day-to-day activities gained, the team was able to create more time and slack to work on improving their working practices, as well as increasing the volume of day-to-day work that they were able to achieve while also maintaining quality.

Value proposition

Every job is different but, ultimately, we all deliver value and someone or something benefits from our work. In order to be viable to employ, we need to create more value than we cost the business. This could be through making, selling, providing or supporting products and services, or in an internal role, such as finance, marketing or administration where you support the delivery of products or services. Whatever your job, you create value and benefits to those with whom you work and your customers.

There is a great principle known as the Pareto Principle. This shows that often there is an 80:20 ratio when it comes to delivering value. In the early twentieth century, economist Vilfredo Pareto discovered the 80:20 rule where, in many scenarios, 80 per cent of the value was delivered by 20 per cent of the resource.

The Pareto Principle suggests that 80 per cent of the value you create comes from 20 per cent of your actions.

Value drivers

It is important to identify what factors drive the need for a solution and identify the value expected. Value can be defined in a number of different ways, depending on the desired outcome. At a top level, solutions can be driven by three alternative objectives (see Figure 9.3):

1. Faster – time is the key driver; the solution needs to be delivered quickly.
2. Better – quality is the primary driver; the solution has to meet quality standards.
3. Cheaper – the solution needs to be more cost-effective; budgets are the key driver.

The construction and IT industry use the triangle below (Figure 9.3) to show these three dynamics and claim that only two of the three can be delivered at one time.

Figure 9.3   Value drivers

For example, if you want the solution to be fast and cheap, it cannot also be high quality and a choice has to be made. Goals cannot include all three of these objectives, as one will cancel out another.

Establishing what determines value at a high level informs decision making by setting objectives against goals. These objectives can be used to inform ranking and prioritisation and provide clear performance measures for actionable tasks.

Controls and boundaries

The work we can achieve is governed by the boundaries of our own capacity and the resources that we have available to contribute to and support our work.

Establishing a clear picture of how our work and time is currently structured allows us to measure our capacity and the slack we can create to increase and improve performance.

In order to implement improvements, resources are needed to implement the changes. Resources can include people and their time, cash for investment into materials and systems, and wider supporting service and support providers. Identifying the resources available, and therefore the constraints of work, is vital to ensure that options are viable when being considered.

Activities have to provide a return on investment that is profitable to be sustainable: that is, that it creates more value than it consumes. If activities are successful, the result of this is that they should generate additional resources that can be reinvested into additional growth and improvement activities.

10. Agile options

> **KEY LEARNING POINT**
>
> Discover simple ways to map out your early choices with the information you have available.

Once there is an understanding of the goal and the reality of the current situation has been analysed, we are in a good position to begin to map out the various options available:

- What are the options for moving from the current reality towards your goal?

- Are there alternative options to be explored?

- Why is this better than the existing/other solutions?

- What impact would each option have?

- What are the key elements of the options?

- Are the necessary skills/knowledge available?

- How does this option impact on dependent activities or people?

- What resources are required?

- Constraints – does the project have any limitations, obligations or restraints?

- Definition of success – what does success look like?

- What are the strengths and weaknesses of this option?

A good way of thinking through the options is to map them out using sticky notes and create a roadmap of the different directions and routes you might take towards a viable solution.

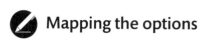

Mapping the options

Draw a horizontal line on a large piece of paper to create a timeline. If you do not have any large paper, use a table, a blank wall or a window or, if you would like something more permanent, a magnetic whiteboard.

On the left, where the line starts, put the current month or year and, at the end of the line on the right, put a date when you hope to have completed your project, reached your goal or overcome your challenge.

Using sticky notes, add the actions you think you will need to carry out and the milestones you might reach on your journey between now and the date you have set. Place these along the timeline.

As you think of actions to add to the timeline, you may wish to move or add others, you may find you have alternative routes to each option. Capture and map these, and draw new lines to show decision points, if needed.

Consider where key decision points may occur: where your path may split and you will have to choose one course or another, and where on the journey these may occur. These forks in your journey may signify places where you will need to decide whether to persevere or pivot in a new direction, which could be a minor or major change.

By thinking through and mapping the options you may identify assumptions to be validated and it may uncover scenarios you have not considered previously.

By doing this, you are gaining a clearer image of whether your journey is fairly easy to predict or if there is a large degree of uncertainty. For the first, agile can help you to navigate efficiently along this fairly certain path but, with metrics and measures, check you are still on course and your actions are valid. In the second, it helps to show you where there is uncertainty and helps to identify the actions necessary to learn more.

Of course, we need to be mindful that along our journey, external and internal factors are likely to change, which may influence our direction and the actions we can take. We may also identify that our initial conclusions may be based on a number of assumptions, and this is our best guess at what it may look like at the start of our journey.

As mentioned previously,

journeys are often like a game of Snakes and Ladders in that we do not know what shortcuts or setbacks we may land upon on the way.

This is a great exercise to do with your colleagues or your customers to help gain context, understand assumptions, identify ideals, consider uncertainty and identify options to progress. Each option can be reviewed and the costs and benefits of each option discussed to identify which should be taken forward.

11. Agile way forward

KEY LEARNING POINT

Explore how to develop a test-driven route to success through observation in order to gain better awareness.

It is important to '**think big**', as it gives us clarity over the problem we are trying to solve, the value and benefits that a solution will bring, and we may even have a clear picture of exactly how that solution will look and function. But the world changes every day by the time we have fully implemented that solution, we may be out of date and the problem may have altered its impact to a greater or lesser degree so it is better to '**act small**'.

So, what we think, or even know, will work now may not be sufficient by the time we have finished the job. By releasing early work for feedback, we should be able to identify change sooner and respond appropriately, as well as deliver value early.

- Which is the preferred option to take forward?

- Are there any actions to be taken before an option is chosen or progressed?

- What metrics can be used to measure success?

Agile is a test-driven development methodology; it aims to validate success by verifying assumptions and measuring acceptance as early as possible into the creative process. This is achieved by continuous releasing and integration and gaining feedback until a point of satisfaction and success is met. Our work has to integrate with our day-to-day working and improve satisfaction, and so we must understand how our solution integrates into an existing environment in which it resides before we can know if it will be successful. Systems thinking helps us to understand connections and dependencies, ensuring solutions are compatible with the wider environment.

Systems thinking

> 'Systems thinking is the process of understanding how things, regarded as systems, influence one another within a whole. In nature, systems thinking examples include ecosystems in which various elements such as air, water, movement, plants, and animals work together to survive or perish. In organizations, systems consist of people, structures, and processes that work together to make an organization "healthy" or "unhealthy".
>
> Systems thinking has been defined as an approach to problem solving, by viewing "problems" as parts of an overall system, rather than reacting to specific part, outcomes or events and potentially contributing to further development of unintended consequences. Systems thinking is not one thing but a set of habits or practices within a framework that is based on the belief that the component parts of a system can best be understood in the context of relationships with each other and with other systems, rather than in isolation. Systems thinking focuses on cyclical rather than linear cause and effect.
>
> 'SYSTEMS THINKING', WIKIPEDIA, 2014 (Available under the Creative Commons Attribution ShareAlike License)

Assumption-driven development

When we have an idea about a new project, product, way of working or option that we would like to progress, we can be driven by facts and assumptions. We can interpret what is going to be involved through experience, gut feel, evidence, what we have been told or in numerous other ways.

We need to validate our ideas and assumptions as quickly as possible. We can do this more easily if activity is broken down into slices of work that can be produced, released and integrated quickly to gain feedback and validate the options. This provides a staged release process that provides the opportunity to reflect on the results and make changes, based on our learning before all resources are spent.

Where we are working on something new and unpredictable or uncertain, this experimental approach enables a measured and informed method. Often we have finite resources to achieve an outcome: cash, time, people, equipment, etc., which can deliver the features that will create the value and benefits desired and be accepted as fit for purpose. We can reduce risk by taking an iterative and integrated approach to solving problems and developing new ways of working. The cycle is continuous and aims to achieve continuous improvement through repeating short activity cycles with regular integration, followed with periods of review where we can observe the outcomes and make decisions based on what this tells us.

Test-driven development

Test-driven development is the name given to a method of software development developed by Kent Beck (http://en.wikipedia.org/wiki/Test-driven_development). The methodology is based upon measuring requirements and acceptance through observing outcomes when work is integrated into existing structures and practices.

Performance and progress is measured by feedback gained from testing the solution against success metrics, and used to inform what further work and change is needed to deliver the value needed and fit with existing systems.

This form of decision making requires that those people or activities that use or depend upon the solution are engaged in the development process throughout, providing the feedback and information needed to establish what is and is not effective, and adapt accordingly.

The benefit to continuous testing through interaction is that we can iden-tify practically if the option is viable to progress, and gain feedback to test the requirements and needs rather than accept what has been said is correct and true.

Behaviour-driven development

> *'If I had asked my customers what they wanted, they would have said a faster horse.'*

This quote reportedly was made by Henry Ford when talking about the adoption of his motor car. The reality of a motorised vehicle was not even an option in his customers' minds; his product was a new option for travel that he needed to prove was viable and attractive.

What we think we want is not always what we want, because **we do not know what we do not know**. It is important to test out our solutions on those who will be using them or those who are reliant on them, so that we can observe behaviour as well as listen to verbal feedback to identify if a solution works.

There was a period before the Model T Ford was mass-produced. The first Ford cars were bought by innovators and early adopters who were willing to consider a new and different option. By sharing our solution in the early stages with those who are eager for improvement and change, we can gain the feedback needed to refine and scale our solution to fit. If feedback is sought only at the end of the process, nothing can be done about it. When we are working on something new, we look to make iterative improvements, testing as we go and tweaking our solution as needed to best fit those for whom we work.

A key benefit to taking a test-driven and iterative approach is that value is delivered early, so the user gets to gain value. They also get to see the development of the solution and therefore get accustomed to it more easily when it becomes normal practice, by providing an incremental delivery process. Rather than having to accept and adopt something overnight, the users get used to seeing and using the solution in stages. This means that there is time to absorb and become familiar with the product, and prepare for integration and manage change over a period of time.

Behaviour-driven development is the name given to a method of software development developed by Dan North (http://dannorth.net). The method develops test-driven development as a measure of success further by focusing on needs, benefits and value, as well as the delivery of a specified feature to achieve acceptance. This allows an element of flexibility in how the solution is delivered and enhances the ability for developers to deliver innovative solutions that are fit for purpose and meet the needs of the client. Behaviour-driven development aims to develop working solutions that can be tested for acceptance by observing behaviour.

'Think big, act small.'

12. Continuous delivery

KEY LEARNING POINT

Learn how to change to a rhythm that works to sustain and manage performance.

Continuous delivery is a concept developed by Kent Beck (the developer of Extreme Programming). It is a software development method that encourages frequent releases and continuous improvement. By working in small rapid delivery cycles, we are able to achieve a state of continuous delivery. Value is delivered early and improvements are integrated continuously through testing and feedback. A small, but valuable, solution is delivered as soon as possible and then the solution is extended, deployed and adapted as needed in small incremental improvements (see Figure 12.1).

In essence, there is no start and end to an agile project or improvement process; the activities continue and evolve from one stage to another, based on the value and return they are delivering.

The idea is that something is never finished because the world continuously changes. For example, a website may change on a daily basis, features can be added or the whole site may be migrated to a new platform, but the project and process is an ongoing one: a business is unlikely to be planning a time where their website will end and not exist anymore. Of

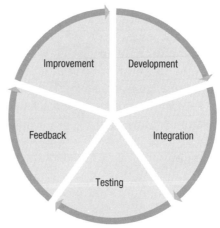

Figure 12.1   Continuous delivery

course, things do end. Everything has a life cycle. Continuous delivery is about bringing in new features and fluid change that keeps momentum and flow consistent. If the process or activity no longer serves a purpose or delivers value, it is likely to morph into something new. Agile allows us to navigate this change and carry over learning and assets of old systems, instead of starting from scratch each time.

Continuous development

Rather than thinking of something as having a beginning and an end, we need to think of them being part of one continuous development of an inter related system, like a cog in a clockwork mechanism. There may be periods of inactivity or snoozing, but the development remains open, unless it is actually closed down or ended. However, even in cases where it appears that something is coming to an end, it actually may take a new form or be passed to a new owner, in which case agile can help with this migration or exit.

Continuous integration

Most activities are linked to another in some way, so changing one work-flow can cause an effect in other areas and, therefore, impact on others' work as well as our own. Continuously integrating our work in progress at regular intervals can help to identify these dependencies, ensuring they are considered and coordinated as part of the solution.

Continuous testing

Testing regularly provides the opportunity to measure the success of work in progress, to test assumptions and perceived value. By testing early we can identify if information is correct, that things are working as expected. This allows us to identify early if our solutions are likely to work and helps to de-risk. Outcomes provide feedback to gauge whether work is on track and fit for purpose.

Continuous feedback

Testing regularly provides rapid feedback on progress and performance against the goals and objectives. Acceptance can be evaluated by observing behaviour and levels of satisfaction. Feedback works both ways and keeps others informed of what is happening, what they can expect, allowing familiarity with the solution before they need to work with it or use it. Continuous engagement additionally helps to build trust and confidence in the solution, improving the likelihood of buy-in and acceptance of the change.

Continuous improvement

Using the feedback and insights gained, we can improve our approach continuously to the solution, taking into account the knowledge and experience we have gained from previous cycles of development.

Achieving continuous delivery and releasing work early for feedback provides us with a test-driven approach to achieving results. By monitoring results and progress regularly and engaging with the wider environment, the solution is developed and maintained.

Being agile and agile thinking outline the characteristics and benefits of an agile approach, and the iterative structure of learning, action and reflection to create agile behaviour. The next sections provide the tools to take workload practically and organise it into an agile structure, using and building on the notes that you have already created in previous exercises.

Part 3

Agile approaches

13. Agile scope

> ## KEY LEARNING POINT
>
> Adopt an approach that manages variables and works to deliver benefits rather than fix and control requirements and the end result.

The agile, lean and coaching tools in the next sections will help you to manage the activities you have mapped onto notes so far. This will help you to track the balance of your workload and measure progress. Agile is a method that focuses on managing and organising your workload as you work, rather than as a separate activity.

Using GROW to establish a clear understanding of the goal, the current reality and the options going forward, the next stage is to break down the work involved into manageable, and then actionable, requirements that can be prioritised and scheduled.

With an expectation of change and evolution of the requirements as time progresses, it is impossible to know and define everything from the start. What is necessary at the start is to get a good understanding of what each of the potential options might involve and areas that might prove difficult, so that we can establish if these are viable as early as possible. If, for example, one of the key requirements would be incredibly costly to implement, it may be that we test that assumption and validate these costs as one of the first activities.

Initially, we want to map out what we think is involved at a high level and make initial estimates, and then refine this over time. As a better understanding is gained, we can refine these estimates and make better informed decisions. Work can be broken down more easily as it becomes a priority, rather than trying to define everything exactly in micro detail from the start.

Starting with the basic plans enables more flexibility as work progresses. As the solution begins to develop, decisions can be made on the detailed elements and which changes are required.

Agile provides an adaptive approach to delivering solutions, based on current scenarios and needs. Initially, there may be a need to act quickly and identify changes we can implement quickly and easily in order to adapt and improve current outcomes. By mapping these current and future activities, we can begin to structure the work we do visually and identify these requirements.

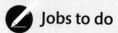 Jobs to do

Building on the notes you have already created, start to map out all the current jobs you have to do, including what your role involves and for what you are responsible.

- **Core jobs** Map the jobs you do regularly as part of your working week. For example, selling widgets, making widgets, marketing widgets. Break down the key tasks involved: prospecting, purchasing, planning, organising.

- **Supporting jobs** Map the other jobs that you do alongside your main tasks: record keeping, reporting, team meetings, answering calls/emails, timekeeping and expenses, training, covering others' work, pet projects, workgroups with which you are involved. Capture as many as you can.

- **Additional jobs** Think about the things you would like to do and for which you never get time. What are the things on your list that never get crossed off? If you keep moving something in your calendar, or find yourself repeatedly writing it on your daily list, it is a good sign it is something you should, could or would like to do, but the must-dos keep getting in the way.

Use different colours to represent different types of work or aspects of your job so that you can differentiate more easily between them.

Expect to add to this later as your mind recalls other elements that you may not be able to recall immediately.

Group the notes into different types of activities and review how your time is spent.

If the work is very dependent on others, then a workshop to establish requirements is a good way to map out their needs and the associated activities. Working together will help to establish priorities and what is important, which will feed into how work is structured and what elements should be tested and delivered early.

Working collaboratively with those who are dependent on the work you do can help to ensure that a state of collaborative working is maintained rather than the more rigid contracting and negotiation. By working openly and seeking feedback we can gain the support and backing of those we work with where the flow of information and an improvement of communication creates a better working environment and team culture.

By interacting and observing those with whom and for whom you work, you can develop a clearer picture of what is wanted rather than rely on written documentation and specification. Observing behaviour and questioning assumptions can help to provide a clearer picture of the requirements and foster a working relationship that continues to provide information that helps to deliver a more acceptable and easy-to-integrate relationship.

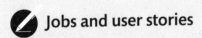 Jobs and user stories

Originally defined by Kent Beck (developer of Extreme Programming) and developed further by Rachel Davis, author of *Agile Coaching*, the purpose of user stories is to establish the current needs of the client, **not** to define the solution. By identifying why the solution is needed and what purpose it will serve, we can see how a solution needs to solve a problem. Unfortunately, often what a customer thinks they want and what they actually need are slightly different. It is only when a customer actually uses a product or service that they are able to identify whether or not it will work effectively.

If you are working on a specific project, mapping user stories is a useful exercise to help map out the job's scope and requirements with those who use, manage or rely upon the solution in some way. User stories set out the different roles and needs associated with the goal, and build up a set of requirements based on benefits for use when developing a solution.

User stories help to establish the reality and the context in which a solution is to be delivered. By defining the user stories we gain awareness of the requirements from different perspectives to gain a greater understanding of what is needed and why.

The technique can be used personally or with colleagues, management, customers or partners to help see and understand the needs of others and how their roles are related. This tool can be used at a variety of levels to identify high-level benefits and gain clarity on minor details.

Establishing user stories collaboratively helps to ensure that needs and requirements are aligned from a number of perspectives, and that there is shared understanding and consensus. Rather than mapping processes and systems, user stories look at the interactions and needs of people to build a picture of what potential scope and requirements are to be considered when developing the solution.

As a [role]
I need to [activity/job]
so that [benefit/gain].

Each user story can be written up on sticky notes and then mapped and ordered so that they can be ranked and prioritised to establish the key requirements.

By working through the user stories we can establish who is dependent on our work and what benefits they need to gain. From this, actions can be established that fulfil the requirements.

Breaking down the scope into jobs is a good way to add context to the solution required: it helps to explore and understand the environment in which it will be used, and therefore be better placed to identify and build suitable solutions that fit the scenario. By establishing the jobs that a user wants to carry out using your solution, options can be established that are more likely to be fit for purpose, since there is an emphasis on delivering benefits and value rather than specific features.

Definition of success

One idea of success can be very different from another, and we need to gain consensus between us and others on the level and quality of work that is to be achieved. It is easy to waste time by doing more than is needed, and cause dissatisfaction from not doing enough.

To help, we can ask simple questions such as, 'What does success look like?', 'How will you know when this has been done?' These questions can help to establish when your work will be fit for purpose.

✎ Definition of DONE

Each activity you have identified can be completed at various levels, from just completing the essentials through to an 'all-singing all-dancing' version. The level needed is defined by those who benefit from your work, and speaking to them about their requirements can be incredibly informative.

Desirable – 'would like to haves' that are beyond the current scope of work.

Optional – added options that could be included if time/resources allow.

Necessary – aspects that should be included to reach satisfaction.

Essential – 'must have' components that deliver a workable solution.

Ranking the scope of work into desirable, optional, necessary or essential components helps to identify if and where they should be developed.

Managed variables

Traditional measures and metrics aim to fix the scope, resources and budgets to enable better control, transparency and predictability of an activity or project. Businesses are always looking for ways of taking out cost and adding value and projects are created based on calculating return on investment.

The problem with trying to pin down these variables is they then become constraints and limit solutions by acting as targets and indicators of success. We need to look beyond fixing the investment from the start, and work towards forecasting and managing what we put in against what we get out on a continuous basis. This does not mean that we get rid of budgets or behave as if we have limitless time and resources, but it does mean that the success of the solution is not measured by its ability to come in on time and on budget; rather, whether it has created more value than it has cost.

Often we experience scope creep: as we learn more about the solution that we aim to deliver, we identify additional work or problems that we need to solve, which increases the scope of work. If budgets and resources are fixed at the start of the work and not reviewed, these changes cannot be accounted for, and a project will end up over budget and consume additional resources that have not been calculated for. This is often where an activity that is identified as profitable quickly can become loss making if the costs and returns are not measured regularly.

The application of resources should be flexible to respond to increase or decrease of value created and adjusted accordingly.

By breaking down work into smaller chunks less commitment is needed to secure time and resources, and so the work does not become overly tied into one specific solution. The method enables flexibility and movement by forecasting and reporting continuously to flag quickly when work may be beginning to cost more or less than forecast, and then adjustments made, or decisions taken on whether the solution is still viable.

Rather than try to fix metrics, such as time, cost and quality, we learn to manage them and, continuously, we still have a goal, a potential scope of work and boundaries in terms of resources and costs. By working in sprints and using the concept of minimum viable proposition (more on MVPs later) we can find out early whether our estimations for what we can achieve with the time and resources available are good, or if we have under- or overestimated.

We also can measure the impact and the value of what we are doing early and, since we have spent only a proportion of the time and resources, we can review and revise future spend and focus.

When we scope out a project, we can end up with more options and activities than we have the budget and resources to achieve. Rather than decide what is in and what is out at the beginning, agile allows these decisions to be made continuously, based on the results we achieve along the way.

14. Estimation games

> **KEY LEARNING POINT**
>
> Learn a series of games that will help you to understand jobs and clarify the expectations of others.

We assume a lot when we make estimations, and everyone thinks differently, so what one person defines and estimates can be very different. The exercises in this section are great to do with your team, your manager or your customers to help you gain a shared understanding of and consensus over the metrics in order to define what is involved in the activity and what the definition of success looks like.

These estimations provide valuable metrics for measuring progress and how accurate our estimations are by comparing them to the actuals. Many tend to under estimate the time it will take to complete a task. Honestly, I think if I admitted how long some things actually might take, I probably would not start them. It is, perhaps, a type of optimism of getting it done quickly and easily, and a tendency to think optimum rather than actual.

There is an old adage in the technology sector that says, 'Estimate and then double it'. Today, some of the largest software companies in the world ask their developers to estimate how much work they can achieve in a given timescale and then they halve this workload, as this is the realistic actual work they will achieve. In the world of software development, there is a high rate of uncertainty and change. If you work in a high-growth business or a sector that is impacted by technology (that is just about all of them, by the way), then this extreme rationalisation of your estimates may be necessary.

By recording these metrics, you can measure how your estimates compare to your actuals and learn to adjust your workload accordingly in future sprints of work. You will also learn when your estimates are likely to be more or less accurate, given the nature of work.

Business as usual will tend to vary less, whereas new activities and change projects will include a degree of uncertainty, but you can be aware of how much you tend to over- or under estimate when estimating the unknown and adapt your rankings accordingly.

Scope creep

Scope creep is a term used to describe the addition of unplanned extra work, once a project has been started. There is only so much that can be defined and planned upfront: as an activity progresses, we learn more about it and so our decisions may change; we might identify that there are elements that were not taken account of at the beginning; or that, due to a change, additional work is needed in order to meet new needs resulting from the change. However, scope creep does not come only from changing our minds along the way; a primary reason for scope creep comes from underestimating how long an activity will take, how much it will cost, how much thinking time may be needed, and additional actions such as rework or hidden costs taken into account that had not been included in initial budgets and estimations.

We can see what work we are achieving and the work that we have planned versus what we did that was unplanned and unpredicted. It is possible to refine forecasts by reviewing previous metrics based on work that we have already completed, and so predict our productivity and manage our performance better in the future. For example, if we become aware that on average, 20 per cent of our work is unplanned, we can build this in as slack in the future in order to take that into account and provide us with the time we need to respond to these ad hoc work requests.

By talking through activities with your team, your manager, your customers and others, you can help to improve communication and gain a shared understanding of how the work breaks down, what is involved, how long that might take and, most importantly, its value.

This is especially valuable if you are working as part of a team and for communicating with your managers and customers, which invariably we are. It enables you to gain better clarity and expectation of what is involved in each activity, as well as a shared understanding of the metrics and priority of each activity.

Estimating helps to give a better understanding of the scope of the work to be undertaken and the impacts and metrics involved. Analysing estimations helps to gain a better understanding of workload and ensure there is understanding across a team about the nature, scale, value and difficulty of jobs, which means there is shared consensus about the work to be carried out and what is likely to be involved.

Working as part of a team and organisation means that each of us is dependent on others both internally and externally. Often, we receive work from one person and then, like a relay race, the baton is then passed to the next. Knowing more about these related activities helps to understand and improve upon working relationships. By estimating the size and time needed to deliver, we can establish what is involved, which will inform the decision-making process when work is being selected and prioritised in the future.

Estimation games

Estimation games are a great game to play with others, especially if there is a need to justify the time that an activity may take and clarify what is involved. The game helps everyone involved to reach a consensus and shared understanding of the work involved and its expectations. This game is derived from the original estimation and planning software-based game Planning Poker™, developed by Mountain Goat Software (used in SCRUM and XP Software Development and first defined by James Grenning in 2002 and trademarked by Mike Cohn of Mountain Goat Software), and has been adapted and evolved for more general use.

The practical outcome of the game is to agree on how the task will be carried out and how long this is expected to take.

- As a group, agree a scale of estimation that you are going to use – for example, one point might equal one minute, one hour or one day, depending on the general size of activities involved.

- As a group, select an activity that has been captured on a sticky note and have a few minutes' open discussion.

  - What elements does this activity include?

  - Who will carry out the activity?

  - How is it going to be approached?

  - Are there other dependencies?

  - When will the activity be done and fit for purpose?

- Privately, each member of the group writes down clearly their estimation of how long this will take on a new sticky note or a piece of paper.

Once everyone has written their estimate, all players show their estimate at the same time.

- Each player then takes it in turns to explain their estimation, what it includes and/or does not include and their reasons for the points they have allocated. The group discusses the variation and the reasons and agrees on a better definition of that task.

Reasons for differences in estimations:

- Different people doing the task, due to different levels of experience, can help to see who is best to do the job, based on how long it would take them, although there is also capacity to consider.

- Different ways of completing the activity.

- Definition of success, or the definition of 'done' for an activity is different – perfection versus good enough.

- Different assumptions of the elements of the process. For example, some may not feel that pre-work or post-work is included and estimate only the actual task.

- Waiting time gets included – the task is estimated in terms of how much time will pass rather than how much time it will take. If there is a waiting time within a task, it is a good indicator that that task needs to be broken down into multiple tasks that have dependencies and can be actioned when needed, rather than staying in an 'in progress' or 'waiting' status for extended lengths of time.

If estimations match, then this estimation is deemed to be the estimated time that the activity will take and it is agreed, as consensus has been reached and the next item is selected.

If the estimates vary, the variations are discussed and then a second and third estimation game can be played, if needed, in order to reach a level of understanding where consensus can be reached.

If difference continues, and an average is not agreeable to all in the group, 'park' the activity for estimation later in the meeting, as a review of other items may aid the decision. Alternatively, it may be agreed that further information is needed before a considered estimation can be made and its size is set.

As an activity is progressed and completed, actual time spent can be captured and the total time spent compared with the estimate when reviewing in order to see if the estimations made were good, or if they had been under- or overestimated significantly. The reason for this can then be established and acted upon in the future.

Estimation games are a great way to help the team gain consensus over what is involved in activities and how long they will take to complete. It helps everyone to gain a better understanding of the level of work that is required and gain a broader understanding of the scope of the work.

Packs of playing cards are available online which have numbers for esti-mation on them: for example, series of numbers such as 0, 1, 2, 4, 8, 15, 40, 80, 100+. These packs often include other cards, such as ?, for when a question needs to be asked before an accurate estimation can be made, or a */joker to challenge the activity. The 100+ card represents a task that is too big to be estimated accurately and needs to be broken down further.

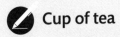 ## Cup of tea

Here is a simple example to demonstrate how estimation can vary greatly. It is great to play with others as an initial estimation when first introducing the game.

I have used this example time and time again with teams and workshop groups and, every time, the outcome surprises its players and helps them reach a new level of awareness and understanding about how we all estimate and assume differently.

Using a points scale of 1–100, where 1 point equals 1 minute, ask the group to estimate the task, 'Make a cup of tea'. Ask them to write the number of points they estimate and, when everyone is ready, reveal estimations at the same time.

The results likely will vary from 1 to 15, and there will be a number of reasons why:

1 – Make a cup of tea for myself, assume I am in the office and have an instant boiling water tap and all ingredients to hand.

4 – Make a cup of tea for everyone, assuming at I am at our current location, knowing that I have an instant boiling water tap so it will not take long.

6 – This is how long it takes to make and drink a cup of tea.

8 – Make a cup for everyone and assume that not just tea is wanted, so it might take a while.

15 – Make a cup of tea for myself, check messages, have a chat in the corridor.

Notice how each estimation has differing assumptions about what the task involves and whether resources are available. Some add additional tasks they feel are part of that process, and some expect change and therefore account for that time. Some assume automatically that it is for them, others include everyone in the group. Almost always estimation is made based on how long it would take them to complete the task.

This simple exercise highlights the realisation that we all think differently and, if estimating making a cup of tea can vary so greatly, then the jobs we do in our work and our understanding of what is involved are also likely to be varied.

15. Ranking priorities

> **KEY LEARNING POINT**
>
> Learn simple ways to establish the importance and order of jobs that need to be done.

The agile methodology works in such a way that priorities are established by analysing the estimations of size, difficulty, value and their importance in reaching goals.

Often there is more work than resources and budget available, so decisions need to be made on what proportion of the work can be completed and what work can be discarded or parked for later activities when time and resources allow.

To help develop and prioritise actions that have been mapped, we can use the user stories and estimations to help establish the importance and priority of the action.

- Does the activity take you closer to your goal?

- Does this activity provide a vital validation/learning opportunity?

- Is the activity urgent?

- How important is this activity?

- Does the activity create value?

When we are in a state of extreme change, our priorities may need to be refactored continuously to take account of constantly moving goals or requirements. Working in short sprints, and using reflection and learning to provide feedback, we can re-prioritise and action the most important and urgent tasks required in the 'next time' box of activity.

If the activity is not taking you closer to your goal, providing useful information or is considered urgent or important, the value of the activity should be questioned and a decision made about whether the activity needs to be done at all.

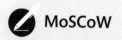

MoSCoW

Adapted from a model developed by Dai Clegg, MoSCoW is an acronym used to help rank the importance of tasks and activities. Use this to prompt activities that you must, should, could or would like to do in the future.

Must have is an essential task, feature or activity that is vital for the project to be successful. It may not be urgent or a priority, but it is important.

Should have is a necessary item that the project should include in order to provide a satisfactory solution.

Could haves are items that the project could include and may add value. They are optional items.

Would like to haves are desirable features that are seen as adding value but are not vital. These might be new ideas that could be very innovative or game changers, and so should be given time for discussion and priority, if desired.

By ranking each activity as a must, should, could or would like to have, provides information on importance and so informs the decision-making progress on what should be delivered early and, potentially, what can wait until later. By establishing the highest priority and value items, this can help to identify the order of development.

There should be a balance of activities within the project: too many **must haves** can increase the risk of the project, as it increases the amount of complexity and number of dependencies, making for an over-complicated solution. Equally, too many **would like to haves** could flag that there is a large amount of new untested work that has not been tried before. This work would require additional validation and learning in order to develop a viable solution, so additional resources and slack to allow for change would need to be built into the scope.

An example of an important **must have** that is not urgent, is a simple invoice; it is an essential component of delivering work but, generally, is not issued until work is complete in the later stages of the pipeline of delivery.

The 'W' can also be defined as 'won't have' when work needs to be cut down.

Value provided

To help establish the priority of activities and refine the work to be done, each activity can be ranked to identify the value it will deliver against the earlier identified goals and objectives. For example, is the goal to be faster, better or cheaper than before?

Ranking each activity against the measures of value and success can help to establish whether the size of the activity is in line with the value it will deliver. At the extreme, if the activity is seen to deliver a high return with little action required, then this would be of the highest value. Large activities that do not contribute to the goals and objectives would be ranked as low. The value of the activity in relation to goals and objectives will help to inform prioritising and planning decisions.

Visualising priorities

To help see the ranking and estimations, notes can be structured to capture a short description of the job/activity, its estimated size, importance and value. A simple approach is to put one in each corner of a job/activity card (see Figure 15.1). You can differentiate types of activities by using different coloured notes or labelling with a category or type.

Visual notes for jobs are useful to provide a high-level overview of that job. The description of the activity and the information on the note are short

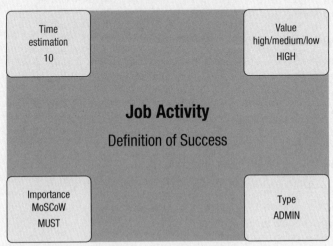

Figure 15.1   Example of a job/activity card

and concise and acts as a reminder and memory trigger when reviewing and planning.

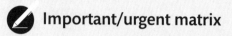

Important/urgent matrix

When activities have been defined and estimated, this provides the additional information needed to be able to rank and batch them into the order in which they need to be actioned. The important/urgent matrix (see Figure 15.2) is a simple tool to help prioritise work, developed by Stephen Covey. Mapping the tasks onto the grid can help to define what might be included in early work and, as time progresses, what can be actioned later and what elements are optional.

By estimating and ranking requirements and by combining metrics of size, value and importance, we can begin to rationalise expectations into a viable way forward to provide a solution that meets needs within the scope and constraints of a project.

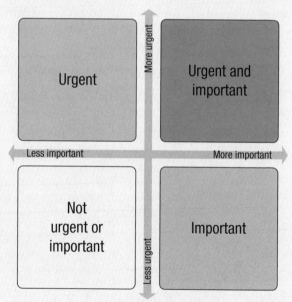

Figure 15.2 Urgent/important matrix
Source: Covey (1989)

16. Minimum viable product (MVP)

> **KEY LEARNING POINT**
>
> Learn how to explore and develop your ideas and validate their viability rapidly.

The minimum viable product (MVP) is a concept (first coined and defined by Frank Robinson within software development) that helps to identify and scope the minimum viable activity that initially can prove, and later deliver, the benefits required to achieve a viable solution.

A key component of an MVP is that while it is minimal, it is also viable; the solution must be viable in that it adequately represents the value. This may be the overall goal, a specific feature or component where more insight is needed. An MVP is not a cheaper or diluted version of the final product; it is a representation of it, either in whole or in part, that delivers value or represents the tangible activity or solution in some way.

Rather than trying to do everything, an agile approach looks at what the MVP might be, so that a relatively small amount of work can be undertaken that then can be reviewed and improved upon. The ideal early MVP is able to showcase and test the solution without doing a lot of work, so that the concept can be tested and proven before further resources and costs are committed. The MVP should validate if it provides a better solution than the current alternative and will be an attractive and viable option.

This concept can be used to test ideas and, as an ongoing approach to developing solutions, the benefit of using an MVP approach throughout development is that time and resources are retained, allowing for staged development, which itself allows the scope to change. By delivering value early, it also means that a return may be gained much earlier in the development cycle, which can be reinvested into additional time and resources for further development.

An MVP helps you to learn more about the scenario and identify whether a particular approach or solution is worthwhile, and whether it should be developed further or not. It is a great way to test your ideas at the start and validate any assumptions you might have, as well as verifying the information provided on which you are making decisions.

Early on, when a goal or a solution is identified of which we have little or no experience, early learning is a key action to finding the best approach as fast and as efficiently as possible. An MVP approach helps to reduce the associated risk by validating and testing assumptions, value and expectations. At this stage, the MVP is purely a representation of the final solution that can be tested to validate the concept and the value it could deliver. By creating a minimum viable product, tests can be carried out to identify if the chosen option is the best choice and if amendments need to be made.

Agile provides a framework to act and learn fast, whether initial concepts and ideas are the right and best thing to progress. Early MVPs provide an opportunity to find out more about the environment and inform our future actions and decisions. The MVP will help you to understand which elements of the solution are of the highest value and which are less important.

By creating an early representation of the solution and releasing it as an MVP, feedback can be gathered that informs decision making in the next stage of development and improvement. An MVP may take a number of forms; it could be a part of the solution or a representation of the solution.

Often, what is thought to be the best option may have unexpected outcomes or consequences when tried. Testing and trialling early can help to identify these and make changes to remove or mitigate the risks identified.

The concept of an MVP builds on the ideals of continuous delivery and feedback, where the definition of the MVP can be repeated to establish the next batch of activity.

By using the initial MVP to record early performance metrics, we can validate and revise our scope and estimations for how long a solution may take and how many resources are needed, and establish early improvements to processes and methods.

The concept of an MVP can be used in various contexts when planning and developing new ideas for growth and improvement.

Three contexts in which the approach of an MVP can be used are:

Ideas – a test to validate needs and value.

Change – quick improvements to mitigate urgent problems.

Solution – a viable solution for delivering value early.

Testing ideas

Using a test-driven approach to solutions development, the MVP is a representation of the solution to be delivered that will test the assumed or proposed value, and provide an insight into whether the solution will fulfil needs and is an attractive proposition.

An MVP is different to a prototype as, typically, this is created before the solution has been developed. The MVP tests should help to define what the initial solution will include and what value it will deliver.

The objective of an MVP is to gain feedback and deliver some value early that can be measured to see if it is attractive and meets needs. The MVP at this stage may not be scalable: for example, the MVP may be quite clunky or time-consuming to undertake, but it is shared with a limited volume.

Quick change

A quick and simple way to solve a problem is to look for small options that quickly can mitigate the impact of a problem, or improve an existing process by identifying simple changes. This is useful especially for improving workflows, processes and systems in the short term that have become inefficient or ineffective. In this context, the MVP works to remove some of the friction or issues that are related to the problem to be solved by implementing small valuable changes.

Quick changes work to reduce the impact of the problem quickly and improve the situation immediately. These changes may be an interim solution or may prove to be a permanent solution.

Viable solution

Often, when a solution is scoped, there are more features and options identified than there are resources and time in which to complete it.

A key aim of agile is to deliver a solution that takes the optimum approach to delivering a solution that is fit for purpose, and satisfies needs enough to be a viable solution for adoption.

The optimal minimum viable solution ideally is the 20 per cent of the solution scope that delivers 80 per cent of the value, as per the Pareto Principle. However, this may not always be realistic and so this theory should be adopted with some flexibility. The MVP solution would be the first release of the solution that would be usable and deliver value, with the use of continuous improvement and delivery to develop, maintain and improve the solution further.

Analysing the work that has been scoped, estimated, ranked and prioritised and the results of any early testing, MVPs will help to plan a way forward and define the initial scope of work to deliver a new MVP working solution.

The minimum viable solution is not just all the 'must have' actions: just because something is an essential must have does not mean it has to be actioned first. For example, a new library requires system training on lending books but time available for this is limited. On the first week the team needs to know how to lend out books and receive them back. Since books are loaned for one week, the team does not need to know how to deal with overdue books and related fines until the eighth day, when the first books lent are due to expire.

In this library example, initially the MVP would be to train the team on lending and receiving books, while training for overdue books can be provided during the following week when there is more time available for further training.

Because of the nature of an MVP, the type of people on whom it is best to test are those who would be natural early adopters. The reason for this is that these early testers are less demanding of tried and tested solutions. They are more interested in improvement and added value than efficiency. The adoption lifecycle is explained in more detail in Section 24, Part 4.

MVPs work in all contexts to find the best way forward by working closely with the users and beneficiaries of the work we do, understanding that actions are inter related and dependent on one another. Change in one area impacts on others and this needs to be considered when we decide what activities are needed and what flexibility is needed for change: MVPs can help to identify and take these into account.

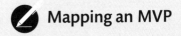

Mapping an MVP

Mapping MVPs is a useful exercise to do when establishing a way forward, both individually or with clients or colleagues. It can be useful especially where there is more work than resources.

Draw three interlocking circles. Label each circle 'Jobs', 'Value' and 'Resources' and fill each with sticky notes with items relevant to that circle (see Figure 16.1).

Value: the benefits that the solution will deliver in order to meet its objectives.

Jobs: the activities/components of the potential solution.

Resources: the resources available, such as cash, time, people, materials, systems.

Move items into where the circles overlap to form potential MVPs that can be discussed and considered. based on the MVP goal:

Test: select the value to be tested and then identify the associated jobs and resources needed to create an MVP to test this value.

Change: select the job to be improved, identify the value that this will deliver and the resources needed to create the MVP.

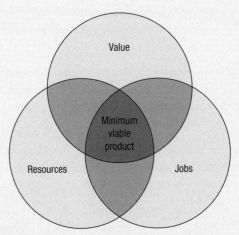

Figure 16.1   Minimum viable product

Solution: the ideal MVP in this context is one that delivers 80 per cent of the value defined by the objectives by doing only 20 per cent of the jobs.

This exercise may create a number of combinations and options that can be reviewed and tested.

Testing with MVPs

Two entrepreneurs wanted to set up a retail online business that generated sales through pay-per-click search engine advertising. The pair had done their research and found two products that received a high volume of keyword queries on search engines, but the competition for these keywords was low. The research suggested a gap in the market for retailing both these products online.

Taking an agile approach, they built their website incrementally in order to test and validate if people would buy Product A and Product B from them, if they were to offer them for sale.

Test 1 – Google AdWords campaign – the team purchased a small volume of pay-per-click search engine advertising for the key phrases and the adverts linked through to a simple website holding page. The team measured if the adverts were clicked on and at what rate.

Test 2 – A webpage with a number of potential product options was set up and, running the campaign again, the team tested if a visitor selected an item for more information and measured the click-through rate.

Test 3 – A shopping cart was added to the site, the AdWords campaign was run again and the basket was monitored to see if items were added to basket and check out was attempted.

Product A passed all three tests and a payment gateway was implemented. The most popular products were selected for sale on the website and the business generated good volumes of sales.

Product B results were poor in both tests 1 and 2. While visitors viewed and clicked on the product options, the rate of attempted check out in test 3 was very low. This low rate of conversion meant that the cost of sales (in terms of advertising costs) was too high and, therefore, the model was not viable, no product was ordered and the website was shelved.

17. Agile dashboard

> **KEY LEARNING POINT**
>
> Learn how to build a practical way to visualise, track and manage your workload easily.

Throughout the past couple of sections you have been creating a mountain of sticky notes and it may feel a little overwhelming or underwhelming, depending on your own personal current situation. This section will begin to give you an agile structure so that you can manage the thoughts and actions you are capturing.

The agile dashboard is a great way to map and track current reality to establish benchmarks. By tracking your current activities using a board you can establish a good picture of the nature and flow of current workload.

To bring order and structure to the volume of tasks created on notes or cards, agile teams use dashboards, sometimes known as a scrum board, sprint board or information radiator. All these boards are quite similar in that they track workflow and can be traced back to kanban, a lean production methodology developed by Toyota (see Section 1) and developed since by David J. Anderson. These information dashboards share the common objective of providing a visual format for displaying workflow in real time.

The nature of agile dashboards is that they contain a number of building blocks that allow individuals or teams to create boards that represent their teams and their workflow.

This allows the boards to be flexible, making them adaptable to a variety of ways and types of working.

In its simplest form, an agile dashboard contains three columns: **to do, doing** and **done** (see Figure 17.1). Actions to be carried out are placed in the **to do** column and then, as tasks are completed, they are moved across the board into **doing** as in work in progress, and then into **done** once

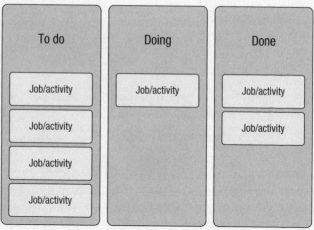

Figure 17.1   Basic agile dashboard

complete. The work in progress box may be limited to a maximum number of tasks and, in order to help improve workflow, the **doing** section can be broken down further to show stages of a specific process.

> ## The benefit of using agile dashboards is that you and your team can gain visibility: it gives the big picture and the detail.

> ## It gets your workload out of your head and onto paper, which allows you to process and manage the information more easily.

The board gives a tangible and visual representation of time and activity. The best way to understand the value of an agile board is to use it. Begin by using it to record your future work, what you currently know has to be achieved, and by adding to it as new work is received. Trying the board out gives an easy and simple way to see practically how the dashboard maps your workload, and shows you the progress you are making.

Mapping work in this simple way can help to identify the different types of work you do, what gets done and what does not get done. If your jobs vary across a number of types of activity, visually grouping different types of work by colour or using 'swim lanes' (rows across the board) helps to gain visibility of the mix of work you are achieving (see Figure 17.2).

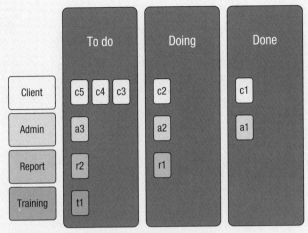

Figure 17.2   Example of an agile dashboard

The board works by pulling the next activity through as the last is completed. Often work in progress is limited to one or two activities; once one has been completed, another can be pulled from the backlog to action.

 ## Creating an agile dashboard

If you do not have a whiteboard handy and, in the true spirit of agile you are very likely to change this board to suit your own workflow, you can start simply with a large sheet of paper, a piece of cardboard, a window or anything of a decent size that will fit a number of sticky notes onto it.

Later, if you find this method to be agreeable, I recommend investing in a magnetic whiteboard or creating a fixed space on a wall or window where your board resides, but for now, just use whatever is handy.

Building on the basic concept of the to do-doing-done board, the board below gives a more structured space that allows you to break down these three key stages further (see Figure 17.3).

A printable version of this dashboard is available at www.beingagilein-business.co.uk.

The board is divided into two vertically: future work and current work.

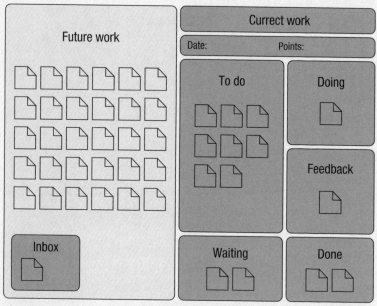

Figure 17.3 Extended agile dashboard

Future work

The left side of the board is for tasks and activities that you would like to achieve in the future, it is the backlog of potential work to be completed. This may represent your working week or month, or it may represent the scope of work for a particular project or goal on which you are working.

Using the sticky notes of actions or objectives you created when you mapped out how you spend your time, or starting afresh, put sticky notes for all the future work you can think of on the left-hand side of your dashboard in **future work.**

INBOX

The inbox is a holding space on the board where new work can be received. As new tasks are identified or handed over from others, these are added to the inbox for review at the next planning meeting. These could be anything from big ideas to small tasks that need to be actioned soon or in the future.

The inbox is a vital element on the board, as it controls the influx of work received and provides a system for managing those requests so that they can be scheduled and planned for. Often work is received ad hoc and can become a distraction or interruption from carrying out the work scheduled. Having this inbox gives a control mechanism to manage the receipt of new work and avoid these ad hoc disruptions. The work received into the inbox is reviewed regularly through board meetings and planning and review meetings, which will be explained in further detail later.

Some inbound work may be urgent and require action immediately. If this is the case, the note or card can be placed directly into the current workflow. However, the volume of this work should be measured and accounted for during planning. For example, if on average four hours of work a week is received ad hoc, then this should be accounted for as slack. Another example would be, rather than scheduling 40 hours of work, 36 are chosen, leaving slack for the 4 hours of work likely to be received that will require immediate action.

In the future work area of the board, you might have ideas or specific tasks: they might be 10 minutes' work or so big you do not know how long they will take until you investigate them further. You can organise these sticky notes as you wish. You may like to put the important/urgent priorities at the top, and things that are at the concept/idea stage further down.

Current work

The right-hand side of the board is for your **current work in progress.** It shows the tasks on which you are currently working or need to complete in the near future. For this introduction, we will set this as your next week's work.

At the top of the board are areas in which to record the date of the current-time box of work and the total points you can achieve during that period. For example, if the time box represents a typical 40-hour week of work and a point value represents 1 hour of work, 40 points of work can be scheduled for actioning during that week, minus slack or other time that needs to be accounted for, for unpredictable new work or other activities not shown on the board. By recording estimates and actuals, and analysing these, we can predict more easily the work involved in each task and improve our ability to schedule work that is realistically achievable.

TO DO

The activities in the 'to do' area of the board represent the scheduled work that is to be completed during the current-time box of activity and is selected from the backlog of future work. It is the minimum viable proposition of what work should be completed in the next-time box.

These activities are a subset of future work that has been identified as the highest priority tasks; this helps to control and focus on a batch of work that can be completed in the next-time box rather than draw from the larger backlog of work. This will help to balance the workload among activities, which can be useful especially if you are guilty of the tendency to do favourite jobs often at the cost of not doing less-favourable tasks.

Move tasks from the backlog of future work into the to do box, use the estimations and prioritisation to help identify which group of tasks should be included.

For larger activities that have become actionable, break these down further into sub-tasks on additional sticky notes, so you can move an element of the task into current work and leave the remainder in future work.

You can break it down as far as is necessary for you personally. A short planning session to identify and set the work to be achieved over the next week should be held and others invited to contribute to this decision-making process, if their input is useful.

Most of us have an element of unknown in our jobs: the requests that come from nowhere and need to be actioned immediately or as soon as possible. This is where we need to be realistic about the amount of planned work we can achieve, and build in some slack to the points we can plan to achieve.

DOING

The doing box is for work that is in progress and is being actively worked on. This box represents current activity.

Limit work in progress – it is recommended that you limit the amount of work that you have in progress. You may like to create a rule that limits the total number of tasks; this can be useful especially if often you start things without finishing them!

FEEDBACK

This space is for work that is considered done and needs to be validated as complete. The activity is reviewed and tested against the success criteria established for that task. This could be integrating the activity to check that it works, or getting it signed off by your manager or customer to get their feedback and agreement of completion. Reviewing work before it is established as **done** is needed to ensure that the work is complete and to a satisfactory standard. If the work is not fit for purpose, then it returns to the **to do** column, otherwise it can move into **done** as complete. The feedback received may help to identify further improvements or additional activities needed.

WAITING

The waiting box is a holding area for work you have started but cannot complete, due to delays from another party. Consider each of your tasks in the doing box and identify if there is anything that is blocked and stopping you from completing that task.

When work is in the waiting area it has been held up and further progress is delayed while you are waiting on someone or something before you can continue. It could be that you are waiting on an external party for resources or information needed to carry out and complete the task. Any actions that are blocked or delayed should move back to the **waiting** area.

Visually identifying actions that are blocked from progressing helps to uncover waiting times or issues that affect the flow of your work. These issues that slow down and delay work from being completed can be flagged in the waiting box, so that actions can be identified to free up the task and move it forward.

Another action may be to break down the task further so that some elements can be completed, while other delayed elements move back into the backlog of future work to be scheduled later when the delay has been resolved.

If the waiting box becomes busy, this can flag a key issue with your current processes. It may be that you are not allowing enough time for dependent or associated tasks to be completed and, therefore, they have been scheduled too early. Often a volume of work stuck in waiting can flag that there has been some under estimation in how quickly something will happen.

For example, work requiring input from a third party may have an expectation of being completed sooner than possible, there may have been an estimation that there would be an immediate response on request but, in fact, it takes a week to respond, due to the third party's other commitments and capacity. Identifying this, establishing the reasons behind the delay, can help to find resolutions to this problem, such as agreeing expectations more clearly.

The review of work in the waiting area is an opportunity for learning, so that in future these delays and blocks are expected, and therefore can be planned for, with scheduling altered to take them into account and mitigate any future delays.

DONE

Once work has been tested, checked and signed off as complete, it can be moved into the done box. This is a holding area for completed work that can be reviewed regularly to inform what work is to be pulled through to action next.

When the done box has a good number of tasks in it, compare what you have achieved against what you hoped to achieve over that period of time. Before removing these completed activities, we can reflect on them and ensure that the learning to be gained is not lost. It is also an opportunity to celebrate completion and success.

You can retain these cards for future reference: some may be repeat tasks and so will circle back to **to do**. For example, if you complete monthly expenses, once complete the action will be due again the following month and so can go back into future work.

Many report a great feeling of satisfaction in the physical action of moving the activity across the board and finally removing the activity from the board, either storing it away or screwing it up and throwing it away because it is done!

Your board should always represent your current workload, both present and future, and show you the status of each of your planned activities.

Over the next couple of weeks, update your board as you progress activities and, at the end of the week, take time to review what you have and have not achieved. Think about what has gone well, what you could do better and the current state of play.

Later, in Section 22, Agile reflection, we will structure ways of planning and reviewing the dashboard through stand-up and retrospective meetings that support managing the dashboard day to day and between time boxes of work.

The board provides a tangible tool that helps to manage choices in work that is scheduled and progressed: it provides a transparent way to visualise work and better understand our performance in terms of the rate at which we work, and identify the areas of friction where our work is held up or slowed down.

We can identify the quality of work through the **feedback box** and become aware of when work requires further action and when it meets the standards required to move to the state of **done.**

At a higher level, the board provides a structure with an easy mechanism to see where work is being focused, and ensures that this aligns with the overarching goals so that the direction is in line with the top-level scope and timeline. Later, in Section 25, Agile culture, these higher level roadmaps and plans will be explored to show how agile can be used to link lower level actionable work with higher level goals and milestones.

Tips

UNPLANNED WORK

Capture any significant ad hoc tasks on the board as you do them and make a note on them that they were unplanned and how long you spent on them (use colours or symbols to differentiate types of task/activity).

This activity will help you gain a realistic view of how you are spending your time and help you to plan more effectively in the future.

LIMIT WORK IN PROGRESS

By limiting the amount of work that can be in progress at one time, this helps to focus attention and ensure that work is completed. It helps to ensure that there are not too many activities being started but not completed.

Often, the reason for non-completion can be linked to delays and hold-ups from other dependent activities, either internal or external. The dashboard can help to ensure that work is well ordered through estimation and ranking internally. External delays are flagged in the waiting area – flagging them as an issue – which helps to free up the **doing** box, so other work can be actioned while waiting.

PHOTOS

Keep track visually of your mapping exercises and your dashboard by taking photographs. This is a good way of documenting your progress at a high level.

Write on your notes with in a fine-line marker pen. This way, when taking photos, words are much clearer and the notes can be read without removing them from the board.

COLOURS

Use different coloured notes or pens to represent different types of activity. This helps to give a quick view of how you are spending your time and helps you to maintain a balance of work.

BOARDS

Create a wall space specifically for your dashboard that is in sight and, ideally, in reach of your main workspace. Magnetic whiteboards are the ideal solution, as the magnets can help to secure your notes in place.

INDEX CARDS

Postcard-size index cards on a magnetic whiteboard can be customised to hold the information about the activity that is needed, such as the estimated time to complete.

AVATARS

If you are sharing a board as a team, you can create magnets that represent each person. This might be a symbol or a cartoon stuck to the magnet. This can help when work is being shared on a board, also to differentiate activities if coloured magnets or different sorts of magnets are used.

LEVEL OF DETAIL

The level of detail that is recorded on the dashboard is down to personal preference and how much detail is required, which may take a few cycles to find. Additionally, some tasks may need to be broken down more or less than others, based on their nature. It may be that existing systems fulfil the need to record the detail, such as time recording systems or Customer Relationship Management (CRMs), so the boards maintain a higher-level view, or feed the systems with the information they need in an easy-to-maintain system.

EVOLVING

As agile is used, dashboards can be adapted and evolved to suit your own personal way of working and the processes you follow.

For example, if your work has a number of different facets to it, then you may wish to customise the board to monitor the balance more visually. You can do this by using different coloured cards or by creating 'swim lanes' for different types of activity. This can help everyone to see quickly if a particular area of work becomes busy, and help to manage the amount of work that is committed to or promised.

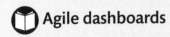 Agile dashboards

Sophie's hobby for making her friends' hair accessories was growing quickly, especially once she started to trade online. After a couple of months, work to do had increased significantly and Sophie's tactic of writing daily to do lists and the long hours needed for the workload was getting overwhelming and felt out of control. Sophie found herself spending large amounts of time trying to keep track of everything and organise and plan her workload and day's work, but with so much to do and little experience in running a business and producing volumes of product, it was hard to know what to do when.

Sophie adopted a simple planner, which allowed her to keep track of her activities and her thoughts as they happened. Simply getting the information out of her head was valuable in itself, freeing up her headspace to think rather than retain and recall. She also colour coded the different activities on her planner to help her keep track of how she was spending her time. For example, on production, marketing and administration, this allowed her to become aware of what work was not getting done, either because she was avoiding doing it, or because it was blocked for some reason.

Sophie also estimated how long she felt each activity would take her, as well as considering if she could break it down further to help get things done in small chunks, rather than dedicating whole or half days to them.

Sophie also created a space for dreams, where she could capture ideas and thoughts that struck her during the day. This allowed her to ensure that the activities, both short-term and for the future, were not lost. Over time, Sophie adapted her dashboard to suit her working style and improve the flow of work. She created a section for growth activities, such as sending out samples to those she would like to work with, and desirable activities that would grow and expand her business and fulfil her ambitions as a creative designer.

Digital options

The physical boards work very well; they are tactile, tangible and visible all the time. However, if you work in a distributed team or rarely are you in one location, a digital agile tool may work for you.

Digital tools for agile are emerging and developing, but are still in the early stages. If you find you have too many things on your board, think about using the board at a higher level and using your existing computer systems within the organisation for managing the detail. Remember, this is a starting point: we will look to evolve and adapt your use of agile for the right things at the right level for you in the following sections.

- **Post It® Plus** is a free app that enables you to capture and store a map of notes. Once captured, the notes can be moved around and remapped. There are a number of digital note apps where you can record notes directly onto your phone or mobile devices.

- **Trello** is a free app you can download to create a digital agile dashboard. You can also share boards with others to help with multitasking. This app works well if teams are distributed and projects are relatively small and straightforward.

- **Lean Kit and Jira** There are also a number of emerging cloud-based software solutions to create and manage agile working. Lean Kit and Jira are two packages from a number of options that appear to be delivering usable solutions. These can be visualised on a wall-mounted screen or projector. With touch technology now becoming more accessible, these provide a virtual board as a solution, but can be expensive to implement.

If you are keen to adopt a virtual version of your board, when first adopting agile, the MVP approach is to use a physical board and notes initially to help develop your board's structure and get used to the processes before migrating to a digital solution.

For more links to digital tools, visit the website www.beingagileinbusiness.co.uk.

18. Lean pipelines

> **KEY LEARNING POINT**
>
> Visualise journeys and progress and create
> communication channels with colleagues.

Lean is a group of methodologies developed within the manufacturing sector (the Toyota Production System in the 1990s) to help run the business and deliver work on demand and just in time. It aims to deliver products in the most efficient and effective way possible. Lean pipelines provide a different way of visualising workflow, which is based on the stages of work over a length of time rather than blocks of time, as on the agile dashboard.

The primary goals of lean practice are to take out cost by being able to repeat and reproduce things efficiently through an optimum workflow with minimum waste. As well as optimising the flow of work, lean works to add value through continuous improvement of both the product itself and the means by which it is produced. This can also be applied to the phased delivery of a service.

The word 'lean' has a number of different definitions and can be used in a number of contexts. Lean can be used to describe leaning upon something or somebody for support, or, to describe the condition of something where it is perceived it carries little or no excess, or, a process or way of doing something that is efficient and economical to carry out, again with little excess or waste.

If we review these definitions in the context of delivering work, lean would be:

Supportive – a dependable approach that we can rely on to provide support to help maintain perspective and provide insights.

Streamlined – highly efficient with little waste and excess.

Economical – delivering value in the most cost-effective way.

Lean pipelines provide a visual representation of the flow of work: the boards show what stage a product, project or customer is at within a defined journey. This could represent the production of a product or a customer journey that progresses through defined stages of work from start to finish (see Figure 18.1).

At each stage the item has a status of **to do,** which represents work that has been received but not started, **doing** to show current work in progress, **done** when an item is ready to pass on to the next stage, and **waiting** for when an item cannot be progressed due to a delay. This delay might be because there is a wait for resources to become available, or a response is needed in order to progress further.

Mapping work in this way helps to highlight when flow of work may be at capacity, and where bottlenecks or gaps may occur. For example, in Figure 18.1, a number of items are blocked at stage 2, which means that currently there is no actionable work at stage 3, leading to a break in activity at this stage. If the block continues, this will have a knock-on impact at stages 4 and 5, unless the block is released and work can continue to be passed on to the next stage before work runs out at stages 4 and 5.

Lean helps to visualise work to understand systems better, to identify and eliminate constraints, and to find the optimal workflow that meets demand and balances resources. The pipeline is demand-driven, where work is pulled through based on demand, rather than pushed along based on the volume that can be produced. Performance targets are based on current demand, which helps to ensure that we do not over-produce and create unnecessary waste. It helps to coordinate and organise work so that it can be delivered as needed, sometimes referred to as 'just in time delivery'.

	Stage 1	Stage 2	Stage 3	Stage 4	Stage 5
To Do	⬜⬜	⬜⬜⬜		⬜	⬜
Doing	⬜	⬜		⬜⬜⬜	
Done	⬜		⬜		
Waiting		⬜⬜⬜	⬜		⬜

Figure 18.1   Lean pipeline template

Using pipeline mapping can help to break current unwieldy processes or systems into more manageable chunks of activity, helping to focus on achieving better workflows. By breaking work into stages, we can create more economical systems and ensure the best use of resources to meet needs.

Pipelines help to raise awareness of progress and help track and calculate the work that remains to reach milestones or targets. Pipelines also help to forecast when work will be delivered. Lean works to identify and reduce variability of delivery and outputs performance. When blocks and bottlenecks become visible, work can be directed to resolve issues to regain workflow.

Pipelines are useful tracking tools to help identify issues when workload is increasing, and so systems and processes need to scale in order to manage the additional volume of work. If workload increases significantly, existing approaches may no longer be efficient or effective, and change to systems and processes may be needed in order to optimise delivery of the larger volume of work.

If new activities or stages are added to the workflow, tracking can help to identify the impact of that new activity on other areas of the pipeline and help to identify ways to integrate them into the pipeline effectively.

Lean sales pipeline

Even a simple board, like the sales pipeline to help track customer acquisition, delivery and retention in Figure 18.2 can be of great value as a visual aid. A card will move through the board, representing a customer or product, dependent on the stage at which they are currently.

Lean workflow boards work well to help teams hand over work between each other and see what work is coming and how work already completed has progressed. Individuals can see their effect on teams and can see what is next and what happens to their work once it is complete. The use of lean across teams is discussed further in Part 4.

By analysing the work on the board, capacity can be managed, ensuring that bottlenecks or issues that affect one stage of the board can be seen and addressed quickly. If issues that are stalling movement within the pipeline do arise, priorities can be revised to address bottlenecks and return

	Lead	Prospect	Contract	Deliver	Retain
To Do	📄📄📄	📄📄📄	📄	📄	📄📄📄
Doing	📄📄📄	📄📄	📄📄	📄📄	
Done	📄📄📄	📄	📄	📄	
Blocked		📄📄📄	📄		📄

Figure 18.2   Sales pipeline

to an even flow of work. Managing the pipeline ensures that capacity is assigned appropriately to maintain optimum flow.

> **Use of pipelines to track activities, customers or products really helps to provide a real-time visualisation of work in progress: a snapshot of where we are, which we can review and find ways of improving by becoming smarter, leaner and faster at what we do.**

Lean Lego: building the Millennium Falcon

A long time ago in a galaxy office far, far away . . . This is a story about a team of software developers who love Lego and Star Wars, who used lean to build the Lego Millennium Falcon. The manual for the build was 300 pages long, and contained over 5,000 Lego pieces. The team comprised five people.

At the start, the team plunged straight in to the box to find the needed pieces and then put those pieces together. Lego was flying everywhere, as the team tried to find and assemble the first pages of the manual. It went very, very slowly.

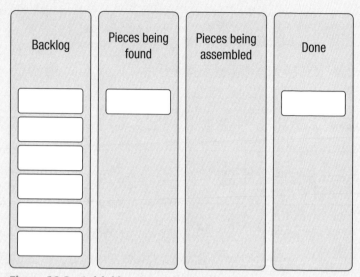

Figure 18.3   Initial lean Lego board

The team mapped a simple lean pipeline to track and measure progress (see Figure 18.3).

This helped the team to model their process and workflow and establish, at the current rate, how long it would take to finish the project, which was 48 hours. This felt like forever to the team and not viable.

By visualising the process, the team could see the constraints, namely finding the right pieces for assembly. This changed the team activities from everyone doing the same thing to the team splitting into two groups: some finding pieces and some putting pieces together. The team formed a queue, with an additional status for when a group of pieces had been found and was ready for assembly.

The team finding the pieces analysed the time it took to find pieces, which varied, based on their size and the number of pieces there were in the box. This varied greatly, but the team were becoming better at finding pieces as time passed and they did it more often. They added a new activity and the finding team began to pre-sort the pieces, grouping the same pieces together before picking them for assembly. This greatly reduced the variability and the time to find pieces, thus making it far easier to collate them ready for assembly, as per the manual (see Figure 18.4).

The team also created sticky notes to identify the pieces they could not find after extensive efforts of searching. Based on the rate at which the

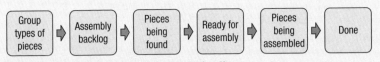

Figure 18.4   Lean Lego optimised pipeline

assembly team were working, the finders filled the pipeline to ensure there were groups ready for assembly, and then switched to sorting the pieces when a number of groups were ready.

They also introduced limiting work in progress in each stage of the pipeline, which they had to, as they could not turn the page of the manual until those had been grouped in piles on the page ready for assembly. So, when all the parts on a page had been found and grouped, or problems occurred that stopped work in progress, the team swarmed around the problem to solve it. For example, if the piece needed to complete the page was still unfound, everyone would work to find that piece.

The time taken to build the finished model was 28 hours and the team were very happy.

Thanks to James Lewis for allowing me to share his story. (Lewis, 2011) You can watch him on video telling his story, complete with Lego action slides, at: www.agileonthebeach.com.

19. Lean efficiencies

KEY LEARNING POINT

Remove and reduce waste with eight commonly hidden inefficiencies.

Agile and lean practices come with a warning triangle because, early on, the method works in such a way that it shows up problems, inefficiencies and deficiencies, whether they are recent additions or age-old problems. Older issues may have inefficient workarounds in place to alleviate the block or delay. At its extreme, these issues can lead to teams feeling like they are in a constant state of failure. As well as helping to identify these issues, agile and lean models work towards ironing out these problems and smoothing workflows. Raising awareness of the problems lean efficiencies provide a method to ensure they are addressed.

By using agile as an everyday management tool, this method ensures that future problems are visible early and, if identified quickly, they usually are easier to avoid, adapt to or solve.

Lean methods identify eight common wastes (see Figure 19.1). (The original seven wastes were identified by Toyota's chief engineer, Taiichi Ohno and the eighth waste – of people or talent – is credited to Norman Bodek, who introduced lean to US manufacturing.) These eight wastes can be applied easily beyond manufacture to help identify opportunities to make savings and provide efficiencies in our work.

Talents

Businesses define their roles and responsibilities based on the needs of the business, which can result in underutilised talents, skills and knowledge within teams.

Empowering people to become self-organising and self-managing through agile structures and methods frees up individuals to focus on work where they add the most value, and utilise their talents to deliver great work that they enjoy.

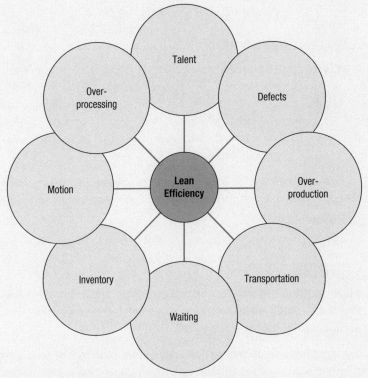

Figure 19.1   Lean efficiencies

Trusting that those employed to do a job are the best people to know how to do that job is vital to ensuring that the skills and knowledge held within an organisation are used to its advantage. Traditional methods control and constrain people from excelling and developing in their careers, and can restrict the growth potential of an organisation.

Defects

A defect is an error or a fault that results in time being wasted, unexpected rework needed or, at worst, thrown away. The defect might be caused by wrong information, poor communication or an error, due to an insufficient standard of work.

Identifying defects and reducing their variability can help to improve productivity. Fixing the defect is not enough; the source of the problem should be found and addressed to ensure that the issue does not repeat itself.

If work is not being produced to the standard required, then there will be a reason for this. It could be a lack of skill or knowledge gap where training or better communication is needed.

The tools and materials needed may be difficult to source, or the time given to complete work may be insufficient. Initially, this may not be a major concern, but the problem may become compounded as more work is pushed into the pipeline, and blocks and delays begin to build until they are no longer workable and change is forced. Seeing these defects and blocks early means we can adapt more easily and quickly to resolve the issue.

By addressing these inefficiencies and deficiencies we can manage and resolve common defects, ensuring that work flows more evenly and without interruption.

Over-production

Over-production is doing too much, producing more than is needed, before it is needed, which can lead to waste and can create a bottleneck, if dependent activities cannot deal with increased volume.

What is produced should not be governed by how much can be produced but how much is needed and the capacity of dependent systems. Work should be delivered just in time, based on demand. By taking an iterative approach we can gauge better how much needs to be completed in order to meet demand. Therefore, output is generated just in time on demand.

Transportation

Transportation waste can be found in movement between people or places. Movement takes time and the less movement, the more quickly things can be achieved.

The time taken for movement between suppliers, partners and customers impacts upon delivery time and can lead to waiting times where activities are dependent on one another being available to progress.

Being aware of where movement impacts upon the workflow can help to identify more efficient ways of transferring between people and places, which helps to ensure consistency and capacity are maintained.

Communication technologies help to reduce transportation of people through tools such as video conferencing. This can save the time and costs associated with bringing people together and so make it easier and more viable to communicate and interact with others more regularly.

Waiting

Time spent waiting extends our timeline. We can look to multitask, reallocate resources, change our processes to reduce waiting times, and look for more efficient solutions that provide us with a quicker return.

The dashboards help to identify areas where work is held up from waiting on something else before it can be commenced, continued or completed. The waiting box and build-up of tasks within a stage are key flags to identify where waiting is causing delay.

If the pipeline of work is not sufficiently fed, later stages can become held up, and the problem can become compounded very quickly. A reallocation of resources to help regain balance within the pipeline is needed, either in the short term or permanently, to address the waiting time and reduce the amount of time wasted. Where waiting times cannot be reduced, processes need to be changed to take account of this issue and ensure that work is managed, so that waiting time is better utilised in the future.

Inventory

Inventory is the stock or resources that you have ready and waiting to be utilised. In manufacturing this refers to raw materials or finished products that are in storage rather than in motion.

Ideally, inventory should be available on demand, but high-value resources can be expensive to keep if they are not being utilised, and difficult to secure at short notice, so it is important to manage this appropriately to reduce cost wherever possible without impacting upon productivity and availability. Excess stock and work in progress can tie up valuable resources, space and cash that could lead to activity being limited in other areas.

Motion

This waste identifies the unnecessary motion that we undertake when we are working. This could be something as simple as walking back and forth to get something when it could be moved closer to your work area.

Reducing the amount of motion needed within an activity helps to streamline the work and reduce the time needed to complete it.

Another form of motion that can impact our efficiency is the navigation of computing systems. The time it takes to navigate and retrieve information can impact upon our productivity. If information is difficult to find or slow to reach, then the number of clicks can be greatly increased. Think of the number of clicks you need to access a document and think of these as footsteps, as with physical movement; unnecessary motion within computer systems can impact hugely on the time it takes to complete a task.

Over-processing

Over-delivering, in terms of providing a higher quality of work than is required and budgeted for, is potential waste and can lead to the value created being decreased. Perfectionism is not always needed; the result needs to be good enough to satisfy only the requirements.

Over-processing and delivering can lead to expectations being raised beyond what is viable. If you always over-deliver, it will become expected and normal. This often becomes apparent if there is a reversion to what has been agreed contractually, where the customer can become unhappy quickly, as their expectations have been inappropriately raised.

There is also the theory of the law of diminishing returns, which suggests that there is a point at which the amount of benefit and value returned begins to reduce the more effort you put in. So there is an optimum balance between work undertaken and value delivered before the amount of effort to improve and refine further is in excess of the value that will be delivered from that effort.

By identifying the point at which the effort put in exceeds the value delivered, we can optimise our resources and outputs ensuring they are firstly viable and secondly deliver the best return on investment.

If the result is that the current effort does exceed the value created then the approach needs to be reviewed, so that it is justified as viable in some way, or an alternative more effective solution is identified that moves it from a negative to positive return.

We can take this further by combining this with the Pareto principle identified earlier which suggests that 20% of our effort returns 80% of the value. By combining the two we can identify and concentrate on the optimum percentage of our work that delivers the most value, and ensure that our work is as efficient as it can be to provide the greatest return on investment.

The Minimum Viable Product model identified earlier can be used to describe this optimum where the MVP is the optimum percentage of work to deliver a viable solution that satisfies the needs of the stakeholders and the value expected.

Agile and lean methods work to uncover and flag waste within your workflow so that you can identify them more easily and see opportunities to reduce waste and, in turn, create a faster and more balanced workflow that delivers the value needed just in time, at a standard that meets the requirements fully.

Workflow efficiencies

As the marketing lead for a conference, I am tasked with taking the raw video footage from the sessions, doing some basic edits and proofing and then publishing them on YouTube.

If you have ever edited video, even in the simplest format for online publishing, then you may already know that a 45-minute video will involve some unavoidable waiting-while-processing time, and watching time. Also, it can take half an hour to save and another half an hour to upload. Then there is time for editing and adding links and details to the website, and notifying speakers' time, so it is an average two-hour job in total for each video. Multiply that by 40 and you will have an estimate of the time I need to commit to this job: 80 hours' work. My time to do this is voluntary, so I need to fit it in between a full-time job and my social life. It is not something I can simply spend two weeks on, like it is a full-time job. I needed to be smarter, leaner and faster.

So, I did a number of things. I reduced the overall time needed by working in batches. I could only edit and save one video at a time, but I could be uploading one to the internet and working on another concurrently. This reduced my estimates of time by multitasking during waiting time. Working in batches and pulling the next video into the workflow, I could work on multiple videos at once.

After my experience of editing 25 videos over three days in the previous year, I was sure that I did not want to take that approach again. But I had learnt, by doing the work as a continuous work in progress, that multi tasking on multiple videos I could process, efficiently and sanely, four videos in around three hours. This efficiency reduced my time commitment from 80 to 30 hours, but still 4 solid days of video processing was not sustainable or viable, given my existing workload.

So, I used sprints to break up the work into sets of four videos in three-hour blocks of time that I would complete in the evenings and at weekends, as time allowed. I could then estimate that I would be able to complete the work in five weeks with two blocks per week.

I was able to set the expectations of the conference attendees about when the videos were likely to be available, and it enabled me to provide a continuous flow of videos over the course of the month after the conference, rather than all at once. From a marketing perspective, this extended our visibility and interaction with our followers and built anticipation for videos that were later in the publishing list.

The process of using an agile approach, and mapping the task on a board, helped me to see the most efficient and agreeable approach to processing the videos. It reduced the pressure I had put upon myself the previous year to complete the process, which had been stressful; it made it more enjoyable and brought about benefits that had not been previously considered. Benefits included drip-feeding the content, which led to extended interaction through social media and email communications and, therefore, increased impressions and visibility during the month. This, in turn, led to a number of additional registrations for tickets for the following year that had not been seen in previous years' sales statistics.

It also allowed me to test and estimate the length of time it would take to process the videos. The conference contained a number of workshop-type sessions, which contained periods of group activity. These videos took longer to edit, as they needed to be watched fully and timings found for cutting the workshop activity from the footage for improved viewing. This meant that some videos took longer than estimated. Another bottleneck was viewing the videos to establish the editing needed. Through natural improvement I was able to adopt a method of scan proofing each session in around half the time of the running time of the video.

From speaker interaction, feedback from attendees and discussions with the conference team, I was able to find out which videos were likely to need editing and proofing more than others, and which were likely to need minimal editing and so could be processed almost immediately. By reviewing my activity, I was able to optimise flow and identify constraints where I needed to become leaner. There is an amazing resource of agile videos at www.agileonthebeach.com. I highly recommend you have a look!

20. Run sprints not marathons

> **KEY LEARNING POINT**
>
> Discover an approach that allows for regular change and improvement while reducing daily interruptions and distractions.

The initial board created in Section 17 enables you to capture your work and track it as it progresses. It allows you to view quickly your future work and pull the next task through as you complete others and as priority requires. This gives you a continuous real-time workflow that you can track and helps you to manage the **act** element of the learn – act – review cycle.

To increase the opportunity to learn and review regularly, agile breaks down a workload into time boxes of planned activity called sprints. Originally developed within software development by Jeff Sutherland and others in the 1990s as part of the scrum development approach, batches of activity are selected and actioned within a set period of time. At the end of the time box, work is reviewed and the next period of activity is defined. These chunks of activity are commonly referred to as 'sprints of work'. A key benefit of working in sprints is that it structures work into short cycles of development and then time, to respond to change, rather than react, at a given time. Instead of the goal being seen as one long marathon, it is a number of short sprints (Figure 20.1).

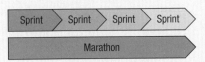

Figure 20.1   Sprints versus a marathon

Agile has established that, rather than work as if you are running one big, long non-stop marathon doing everything in one go, it is better to work in short sprints of activity with time to stop, reflect and plan regularly.

Scope to change

By working in sprints, at the end of each one there is time to stop and review what has been achieved during the sprint, measure the impact and decide what activities are best to action in the next sprint, based on current information. This enables you to make small incremental steps towards your goals, monitor progress and make changes to the future work that has been scheduled. Working in sprints provides the opportunity to review and revise priorities regularly, based on feedback and to change direction if needed.

Work within a sprint is defined through a sprint planning meeting, where time is taken to schedule the next batch of work from the backlog of future work. Typically, a sprint is between one week and three, to allow for continuous refinement and change. The sprint length should be an appropriate length so that planned work can be changed regularly, but not constantly. Regular ongoing reviews of the board and the progress should be undertaken throughout the sprint to manage work in progress and identify any issues that may stop the work from being completed.

Focus and control

Working in sprints can help to control inbound work by using the inbox on your board for the receipt of new work and ideas. To help maintain focus on the work in hand and avoid interruptions and disruption, items added to the inbox should be reviewed in batches, rather than as they appear, which helps to focus on current work in progress.

Ideally, once the work is set for a sprint, this should not change until the next sprint to avoid too much disruption from constant change. If ad hoc work is likely to occur, then slack should be built in: for example, only 30 rather than 40 hours' work per week to allow for 10 hours of ad hoc work. This will help to protect focus on the current work in progress and avoid constant change.

Once a structure of working in sprints has been established, this helps to manage expectations and requests for new work. There is a clear time when change can be considered and new work can be added in-between sprints of work at sprint meetings. This means that, while a sprint of work is in progress, you are able to focus on completing the current batch of work.

By working in sprints, at the end of one sprint, or perhaps two or three sprints, there should be deliverables that can be shared to obtain feedback on progress. Metrics can be reviewed to ensure that work is on track.

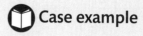 Case example

A proactive and busy sales director of a growing website development company had an ad hoc approach when handing over new work to the development team. Following an increase in volume of work and the growth of the team from two to four developers, this began to be a difficult system to manage, which left the team feeling pressured at times, given the volume of work expected.

The director would walk into the office and announce a new urgent piece of work, and the team would have to abort current work to work on the new project. This meant that other projects became delayed and, as the volume of work being won escalated, projects were started yet fewer were completed. The sales director recognised this as an issue and identified an agile approach as a potential solution.

The team adopted an agile dashboard on a large whiteboard in the office to manage workflow and show the activities of the development team scheduled for the coming week. The team started working in weekly sprints and pulled through a week's work at a time from the backlog of future work, based on priority. The sales director was included in weekly meetings, which gave a channel to pass new work onto the development team. If the work was urgent and given to the team in an ad hoc way, this triggered a stand-up meeting at the board to discuss the size of the urgent task and decide what was to be removed from the board to enable resources to be freed up, so that the urgent project or activity could be completed.

Beyond the improvements in structuring and organising work that the dashboard brought to the team, the dashboard also helped to communicate with the sales director and raise awareness of the impact of ad hoc urgent work on the team and the flow of work. This led him to be more mindful when setting client expectations. By being part of the weekly review at the end of each sprint, he was also able to relay progress back to the customer more thoroughly and regularly. As a result, the team became less distracted and less pressured and, in turn, more productive and happier. As a bonus, since the team were recording their time spent on projects more accurately, they increased chargeable time by 20 per cent to the customer but, overall, reduced the project cost to the customer.

It is better to run short sprints with time to take a breath and compose ourselves in-between them, than attempt to reach our goal in one long marathon.

21. Sanity metrics over vanity metrics

> **KEY LEARNING POINT**
>
> Learn how to set measures that inform and identify development opportunities.

In today's fast-changing business world, measuring impact in real time through agile gives us the benefit of real-time reporting and instant feedback. The purpose of metrics is to inform us whether what we are doing is working. Metrics track success and performance against goals, objectives and targets to establish if we are working effectively.

Metrics should tell us what we are doing well, show us where we can do better and help steer us in the right direction. Good metrics can tell us two key things about the work we are delivering:

1. **Are we doing the right thing?** Measures of success tell us if our work satisfies and meets the needs of its users by delivering the value and benefits needed. These metrics tell us we are on track with our solutions and they are proving to be effective and successful, or not.

2. **Are we doing the thing right?** Performance metrics give us insight into whether the approach we are taking is an efficient and effective approach. These metrics establish whether our performance results in a return on investment: that more is gained than is spent. These metrics help to justify that the results are worth the work and effort needed to achieve them.

Vanity metrics

Vanity metrics are the sort of metrics that tell you only what you want to hear and that look good: they massage our egos and paint a picture of the best parts of the story rather than the whole story. Vanity metrics can be misleading, as often they tell only part of the story and show the positives, which have little value and act as a distraction from what may be happening beneath the surface.

Choosing the right metrics and measures of performance can be the difference between success and failure. Metrics should be informative and reveal opportunities to improve and expose problems and risks to our performance. As well as showing where we are doing well, it should flag areas we can do better.

> 'It would be nice if all of the data which sociologists require could be enumerated because then we could run them through IBM machines and draw charts as the economists do. However, not everything that can be counted counts, and not everything that counts can be counted.'

CAMERON, 1963

Sales vanity metric

This sales vanity metric (Figure 21.1) reports a good volume of leads and a great conversion to prospects, which would suggest that this sales pipeline has good prospects in terms of generating sales with lots of validated potential customers in the pipeline. This metric does tell us that we have a good volume of prospects, but it does not tell a complete story.

If we look at the next phases of the pipeline (see Figure 21.2) we can see that there are only three sales completed and no repeat sales. So, the conversion rate for actual sales is 1 per cent. If the item being sold is a repeatable purchase rather than a one-off, then the lack of repeat sales would be a red flag to the sales team.

The initial metric might work to keep management happy in the short term but if no sales are generated and sales are not repeating, ultimately the sales method in practice is not sustainable.

Leads	Prospects	Conversion
500	300	60%

Figure 21.1　Vanity metric

Leads	Prospects	First Sale	Repeat sale
500	300	3 Conversion 1%	0

Figure 21.2　Sanity metric

If the metrics were to show the entire pipeline, they would show the success of a large volume of qualified prospects, but that those prospects are not converting to paying customers and, perhaps more so, that some of them are not choosing to buy again. Using this information, the team can revisit the activities across the pipeline to establish if there is an issue with the selling process, or if the prospects simply are not the right kind of customer and there is an issue with the validation of a lead to a prospect.

Sanity metrics

Sanity metrics are the measures that tell us what we need to know in order to leverage success and address weaknesses to ensure that we are both delivering the right thing, and delivering the thing right. Sanity metrics help us to identify how much work we are achieving, and what value that work delivers.

Sanity metrics tell us what is actually happening and how we are progressing against our goals and objectives. These metrics are real-time, true representations of the current state of play and performance trends that inform decision making and drive direction for future work.

Metrics should provide ratios and rates that tell us continuously where we are and measure if our actions are having positive or negative effects on the work we are delivering.

Using the sales example, if we are looking to increase sales, a more suitable sanity metric would be to create a ratio of prospects to sales. This would provide us with a conversion rate that can be established as a metric upon which we wish to improve.

The conversion rate can be monitored, as a variety of ideas are tested to increase the conversion rate. A second action would be to test the validation of prospects as genuine potential buyers, in order to ensure there is a product–customer match and that there is demand for the product.

Another example of a good sanity metric is a repeat or retention rate. Many businesses are reliant on customers being retained, as the cost of an initial sale is generally more expensive than repeat sales or intervention because the customer is easier to reach, whereas new customers require prospecting and time to convert.

Social media businesses are a great example of where the repeat metric is vital. It is not the number of sign-ups to the network that is the key metric, it is the number of times that a user revisits and engages on that network that creates the value. Maintaining engagement and retaining customers is key to most business models, and metrics should help to measure this and report if any anomalies appear so that they can be analysed and acted upon quickly.

Measures of success

A key value metric is one that enables us to measure the value of our work against our objectives, which may be to improve our work, making it better, faster or cheaper than before. Results are compared with the acceptance criteria to establish whether our work is fit for purpose, satisfies the requirements and produces expected benefits.

When we measure the value of our work, we want to establish whether we are achieving the desired results. Not all these measures work in harmony with one another and so it is important to clarify what it is being measured against. There is a need to balance our work: if a key objective is to improve quality, then the volume of work we are capable of achieving may drop, as a higher quality of work generally requires more time and resources to achieve.

Releasing work early, using tactics such as an MVP and test-driven development, provides us with metrics that can be measured against our estimations and rankings to establish if we are on target with our solutions, by analysing value metrics through using feedback-driven development.

Value metrics

Review of value can be achieved from gathering feedback on levels of satisfaction, levels of engagement and return on investment. These metrics are not necessarily numbers, and not all value is created at the point of creation or delivery; sometimes value comes later.

An example of indirectly measurable value, the goal of increasing visibility of a product or service to increase sales is a popular marketing activity. Here the goal is to raise awareness of a product or service and, in turn, this creates more prospects to convert to a sale. The value and the benefit are delivered in terms of prospects bringing more potential sales rather than actual sales.

Added to this is the quality dynamic: while the activity has led to raised awareness, the value, in terms of sales, may not change if the people who are now aware of your product are not interested in buying it, conversion rates decrease and other performance metrics report a negative impact. Working this out as early as possible is vital to enable change.

Performance metrics

There are a number of metrics we can use to measure performance against our targets and goals that enable us to see whether we are delivering work that is of the right quality, at the right time, to provide gain and benefits that move us towards reaching our goals and targets.

Performance metrics identify if the value that the work is producing is worth the effort being made. To be sustainable, we must create more value than we are consuming in our efforts and so deliver a positive return on investment.

Metrics also can help to identify waste and opportunities for improving current processes and systems to deliver work more efficiently and effectively.

Volume metrics

A volume metric is the amount of work being achieved and completed, and can be compared to what the initial forecast showed could be done. Identifying if we are under- or over estimating our workloads can help to ensure we schedule a workload that is achievable without the need to cut corners or constantly miss targets.

By measuring the amount of work we are achieving in our sprints, we can start to measure our velocity towards our goal. By recording actuals, as well as our estimations of activities, we can calculate at the end of the sprint how much work has been achieved and gain insight into how we may have to refactor our previous estimates for future work.

As well as reviewing the work that has been completed, it is valuable to look at work that has not been done. A tactic within agile is to reduce the amount of work required by identifying work that does not need to be done in order to reach the goal. This may be taking our wasted time or activity, or features that are expensive to create and deliver low value, or are rarely required.

On average, when using software, we use only 20 per cent of features to carry out 80 per cent of activities – this statistic has led to the development of new software and devices that focus on delivering a limited set of features that still provide a viable solution most of the time. A good example of this is tablets versus laptops: the functionality of a tablet is focused on email, internet and social media, which is far more limited than a laptop. However, because these features make up a large proportion of laptop use, the tablet has become a viable alternative, providing easier and simpler accessibility to these services.

Work not done

Simplicity – the art of maximising the amount of work not done – is essential.

One of the key principles behind agility is keeping things simple. Agile works on the principle that solutions should be built to be fit for purpose. Often, there is a degree of work included in a scope that does not deliver significant value, or is above and beyond the requirements of a solution, and so may not need to be completed straight away or even at all.

If we can establish better, faster, more efficient ways of working, then we can reduce the amount of work needed, and so there will be an amount of work that is no longer required to be completed. Projects often are over-scoped and so, very likely, there is work in the backlog that will never be completed and will be discarded or stored away for future action, should it be needed.

Velocity

Agile enables change with the addition and removal of tasks within the work yet to be done. When we have a backlog of work, and an average rate at which we are completing work, we can map how our work is reducing or increasing over time. With this information, we can track our velocity and predict when we are likely to have completed a volume of work.

📖 Burn up/down charts

Burn up/down charts are popular in software development for showing progress over time and the backlog of work. In this graph (Figure 21.3), a project with 500 points of work has been defined, and the team estimate they can achieve 50 points of work per week. Based on this estimation, the time to complete activities will be 10 weeks. The light grey line shows this average.

The dark grey line shows actuals: in weeks 1 and 2, progress is slow and only 30 points of work are achieved each week; however, in week 3, the chart decreases by 150. There are a couple of reasons for this decrease: the team achieved their 50 points of work, but also, during the sprint review, 10 points of work were removed from the backlog, as they had become unnecessary.

In week 4, the team achieved 50 points of work and were on the path to complete early; in week 5, 100 points of work were achieved, as extra resources had been made available. These extra resources highlighted some issues during the review meeting and a number of unforeseen activities were added, which put the team back behind target. Over the course of the next four weeks, an average amount of work was achieved and some last few activities were discarded as the project came to an end.

Plotting the volume of work onto a graph, we can see the rate of burn down or burn up of work. By visualising the work in this way, we can see clearly the impact of adding and removing work from the workload. In some cases

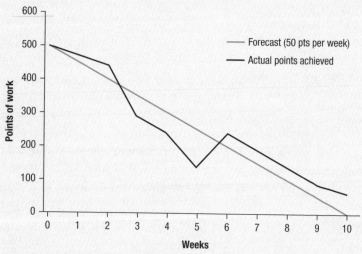

Figure 21.3   Burn up/down chart

work may continue to escalate. If a burn chart is being produced regularly, a trend should begin to appear which will flag that time, and resources will not be sufficient to fulfil the volume of future work in the backlog.

These charts enable you to see the velocity of work in progress and measure this against where it was predicted to be. It can help you to report back the impact of change to the scope of work and the effect that increased, or ad hoc, work has on workflow.

Measuring change

Understanding progress through metrics and visualising the movement of work over time can allow us to pre-empt change and enable us to adapt our practices, not only to improve but also to sustain our current positions. If we do not respond to our changing environment, we can lose traction and momentum.

Change can come from internal decisions or external changes in the environment in which we operate, and both can impact upon our ability to deliver value and sustain performance. By measuring value and performance regularly, it is possible to identify and track trends and changes to the amount of work or the quality of work over time. This can help inform future decision making and identify opportunities for improvement.

If there is a target to scale work and increase throughput, metrics can be key indicators that show where existing processes and systems may struggle with the increased workload and are hitting capacity, or where the increase may be causing a bottleneck or a decline in performance.

One key benefit of digital agile tools is that they can calculate performance metrics automatically and display them in the form of graphics, such as burn down charts, rather than being manually produced. This is a key benefit of digital tools, but has to be weighed against the benefits of a physical board and doing the calculations manually. As with maths and calculators, while the calculator improves efficiency, it does remove the benefit of the learning that comes from working it out manually and being able to see the workings, which can be of great benefit to increase understanding of the metrics and the information they are providing to us.

One solution is the use of touch-screen technology to display boards, which provides a visual and still tactile dashboard while providing the computing power to quickly and efficiently create and display real-time performance metrics.

22. Agile reflection

KEY LEARNING POINT

Explore simple ways to build reflection and learning into your everyday working practices.

Reflection is a skill that is vital for raising awareness through feedback that enables us to learn, and identifying opportunities for improvement and change.

On a day-to-day level, reflection can help us to plan and evaluate work in progress. With each sprint we can reflect on the performance and outputs of that batch of work. By combining the learning, action and reflection from previous sprints of activity, we can review and measure against our goals, objectives and chosen direction to ensure we are **doing the right thing** and **doing the thing right.**

In order to reflect well, we must take time to gather a clear picture of the reality of our actions. The agile approach provides valuable data through the activities of estimation and ranking, and mapping actual workflow, establishing accurate measures that can be reviewed and evaluated.

Regular reflection is interwoven into the fabric of the agile philosophy and methodology, and includes techniques such as retrospective meetings held at the end of each sprint of work (see Figure 22.1).

Time for reflection provides a means to review feedback that we have received from releasing early versions of our solution, which works to inform and guide future work. By regularly reflecting on progress, we can see the impact of our work and how it fits with our environment and its dependencies.

From reflecting on activities and progress, we can identify what is going well and do more of that: we can strengthen and build upon the positives. The flipside is that we can be better aware of what has gone less well and what can be done to prevent underperformance in the future.

Reflection enables a comparison to be made towards our estimation of where we predicted we would be, and the results of our actions against the current reality. We can review our metrics and adjust our projections accordingly. The agile dashboards help to capture and visualise this to see progress, impact and value.

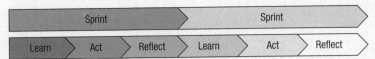

Figure 22.1 Sprints of learning, action and reflection

By reviewing and refactoring every few weeks we are able to evoke lots of small incremental change, which adds up to big change but in a managed and controlled way. Risks can be identified early and decisions made to respond to changing situations and scenarios.

At its extreme, agile provides a methodology to learn fast and fail fast if an idea is not viable, which can save a lot of pain from progressing something that is not worthwhile. Equally, it also provides a format to review ideas that are not effective and to find ways to change and improve them, so that they evolve into being viable and effective solutions.

Retrospectives

A retrospective (a term used in software development to describe meetings that review past performance, inform future work and identify improvements) is the name given to reflective practice within agile. It contains five key questions that can be used to review your whole approach to working as a part of day-to-day reflection of work in progress, sprint reflection for short-term targets, and reflecting on the goals and objectives and direction we have established through our GROW model.

- What is going well?
- What can we do better?
- What is stopping us?
- What has changed?
- What is next?

WHAT IS GOING WELL?

Reflection allows you to identify what is going well and recognise good performance. It is an opportunity to celebrate success and review the impact of positive outcomes in bringing you closer to reaching your goals through your work.

By reviewing what is going well, there is an opportunity to focus on what works and what can be done to harness and grow those elements further. It also identifies areas that are performing efficiently and whether these may be causing a positive or negative impact on related and dependent activity. Often, when we improve one aspect, it requires that another aspect also will need to change or improve to compensate for the impact, which is an opportunity for continuous improvement.

It is really important to recognise success and good performance, as it is all too easy to dwell on the negative and what we do not get right.

WHAT CAN WE DO BETTER?

As part of the retrospective, we look to identify opportunities for improvement by identifying areas of our work or solution that have the potential to be done better. Better, in this sense, may mean better quality, faster or cheaper.

What activities did not go as well as planned? This could be due to a number of reasons, both internal and external. It could be internal, where areas of your work can be improved and developed in order to increase performance and outcome.

Rather than dwelling on what went wrong, or suggesting that something is not good enough, the question is angled to be solution-focused, identifying what can be improved. For example, reviewing lean efficiencies may provide opportunities to identify and review opportunities for improving efficiency and value through reducing waste, and making best use of the capabilities and capacity available.

Externally, there may be an unforeseen impact of integration or changing requirements that mean the planned work does not fit as well as expected. Other internal and external events also may have impacted on your workflow. These may have caused interruptions, distractions or blocks.

If your work is not receiving the good reviews you hoped for, this could be miscommunication, which easily can lead to misunderstandings. Ensuring clarity through retrospectives can help to make certain that you are clear on needs and expectations. It is vital to question and ask for feedback to clarify why it is not satisfactory, so that the next cycle of work can identify amendments and improvements to address concerns, and deliver a solution that is agreeable.

WHAT IS STOPPING US?

Review what is stopping you – where the blocks and bottlenecks are within your work – so that you can act to improve the flow of your work. This can highlight waiting times, gaps and opportunities to improve processes.

Bottlenecks can show where estimates are wide of the mark or activities are under-resourced, and where a team can swarm to help relieve the pressure points by working together. Resources may need to be reallocated, additional tools or solutions brought in to address delayed responses caused by issues with other dependent activities, and actionable tasks should be established, in order to improve the flow of work going forward.

If there is always a waiting time within a particular task it is a good indicator that that task needs to be broken down into multiple tasks that have dependencies and can be actioned when needed, rather than staying 'in progress' or 'waiting' status for extended lengths of time.

WHAT HAS CHANGED?

Being aware of what has changed and what may affect your progress is vital. Are there external factors influencing your environment that need to be addressed? Are there internal changes that impact upon your ability to do your job? How do you need to adapt to take this change into account, and are there opportunities of which you can take advantage?

New work also can be classed as change that needs to be considered. Items that have been added to the inbox or collated on an ideas board can be reviewed and scoped to establish whether they should be added to future work, and where they should be prioritised through estimation and ranking.

WHAT IS NEXT?

The final question of the retrospective is defining what next. The reflection and learning from the previous questions should provide actions going forward for what the next sprint of activity should contain, and any broader actions that are required in order to support the success of the next sprint.

If following the retrospective, changes are needed, these are recorded for action in the next sprint planning meeting. This might be new work that needs to be added to the backlog of future work or changes to current work.

- What should we stop doing?

- What we should start doing?

- What should we do more of?

- What should we do less of?

- What should we keep?

- What should we lose?

- What should we add?

If the retrospectives uncover a potential need for a change of tactics at a high level, or flag a potential change of direction, then the GROW model and scoping and estimation techniques should be used to help map and review the options for change.

The outcome of a period of retrospection should feed into learning, which can inform the scope of future work. It provides the knowledge needed to revise resources, review estimations, reprioritise the future work and map what will be in the next sprint of activity.

Stand-up meetings

The purpose of a stand-up meeting is to maintain a real-time image of work in progress. It acts as a mini-retrospective to review progress regularly within a sprint. Stand-up meetings (daily meetings commonly held by scrum development teams and, more widely, by software development teams) classically are very short, 5–10 minutes in length if there is a team, often just a minute per day, if just an individual.

A stand-up meeting is a meeting where you literally stand in front of your board and update it. Whether working alone or as part of a team, taking a few minutes to update the board every day means the board maintains an up-to-date representation of current status and work in progress through-out each sprint of work. You may invite others to your stand-up meeting. For instance, this may be someone you want support from to help deal with a blockage. Ideally, everyone who has work on the board will join the stand-up meeting.

- What has been done since the last stand-up meeting?

- What did you do yesterday?

- What is currently in progress?

- What are you doing today?

- What are you doing next?

- What are you doing tomorrow?

- Are there any blocks or delays that require action?

The outcome of this meeting is that the board is updated and its status is reviewed quickly; any obstacles can be identified and actions set, if needed, before they impact upon progress towards completing the sprint. Any unresolved issues should be taken to the sprint retrospective at the end of the current sprint for further discussion and agreement on action needed.

These are some signs of delay and blocks:

- I was interrupted yesterday to do something else.

- It is taking longer than estimated as resources/equipment are limited.

- I need a dependent activity to be completed before I can start on that activity.

- I am awaiting a response from an external contact, which I need before it can progress further.

If you are working as a team, the benefit of having very short daily meetings, rather than the typical monthly team meeting, is that focus is maintained. Meeting time is productive in updating the status of work and presenting a view of work that can be reviewed easily to see if work is running as expected.

Another benefit of meeting daily is that it is much easier to catch up if you miss a day. Depending entirely on the scenario, a stand-up meeting does not strictly have to be daily. However, a dashboard should be updated regularly during a sprint. The board should be updated as needed, which sometimes may be multiple times a day; at other times, every other or third day may be sufficient.

 ## Sprint retrospective meetings

Regular stand-up meetings will drive short-term activity and responses to daily influences on workflow. At the end of each sprint of work, a retrospective meeting is an opportunity to review performance and identify change, based on the last sprint of work. The outcome of this meeting will inform the next sprint planning meeting.

A sprint retrospective meeting (the reflective meeting held at the end of each sprint within a scrum software development team) should include those who are actively working on the work, which might be just you or members of your team. You may choose to invite your manager and those associated with your work as appropriate, or indeed customers so that you can update them and gain their feedback.

- What has gone well?
- What can we do better?
- What is stopping us?
- What has changed?
- What is next?

A sprint retrospective gives the opportunity to gain feedback more widely and provides a structure for regular feedback and input from customers and others who are involved or impacted by your work.

By structuring planning meetings to be quick and often, we avoid the need for lengthy monthly meetings where half-day meetings turn into whole days with the result of very little productivity or actionable outcomes. In comparison, using agile takes up comparatively the same amount of time, but structures it to be little and often and driven by specific purpose in contributing to planning and reviewing activity.

Stopping regularly to reflect upon the results of our work means we can see what is going well and what we can improve upon – we can address any blocks or changes and decide what is next.

23. Learning from experience

> **KEY LEARNING POINT**
>
> Recognise that agile methods provide a platform for changing direction as we gain more experience and understanding.

Charged with information and feedback from our activity, we can reflect, learn and decide what we should do next. We have two options: to carry on with our current course of action, or change and adapt future activity. If the feedback received is good, we can continue on the path with the next priorities; if feedback is showing a lack of satisfaction, we may want to change our plans and explore alternative options. We can persevere, carry on as planned, or we can pivot and try something different instead.

Decisions may need to be made about whether to persevere with these activities or pivot and try something else instead. Tracking of performance metrics, comparing actuals versus estimates, helps to see what areas may be lacking in performance and why. Question whether you are the best person for the job, more or fewer resources are needed, or alternative people or skills. Would these actions result in lower costs or perhaps add more value? It may be that learning and skills development is needed to ensure that the activity improves going forward, or that distractions need to be dealt with to regain focus.

Reflecting on the results of previous work and the feedback we gain from releasing our work early helps to establish what is and is not working, and what has been learnt. We can then use the experience to drive decisions for the next cycles of work. During the next cycle, the requirements can be revisited by refactoring, re-estimating and reprioritising the future work previously defined to fit with the feedback and learning gained to optimise future performance.

Before beginning the next cycle of work we need to decide whether to stick to our path and persevere with our plans, or pivot and choose a new direction based on the feedback we have gathered.

Part 4

Agile culture

24. Sharing agile

> **KEY LEARNING POINT**
>
> Discover ways to introduce others to agile: those who will be most likely to join you early and those who may take some time to convert.

In its original form, agile was developed as an approach for teams: a way for software development teams to work together to deliver solutions in uncertain and unpredictable working environments.

Agile is a simple way to visualise and structure work and get everyone involved on the same page. The same techniques, tools and exercises for individual adoption of agile work very well across teams and organisations.

Sharing tips

- Use sticky notes to facilitate and capture key points in meetings.

- Create an ideas cloud in the office where the team can write suggestions.

- Introduce colleagues to your board as a way of knowing what you are doing.

- Facilitate an agile tool in team meetings: estimation game, MoSCoW, DONE, five retrospective questions.

- Create an agile board as a snapshot in time for a specific project or workflow with colleagues to help gain understanding.

By using agile in your normal day-to-day activities, there will be a natural introduction as you use these tools to communicate with your colleagues about mutually relevant work. Agile tools are a useful communication aid when you are discussing joint activities or ones that impact upon others in some way. If you are working with others on a particular project, the agile method can be used to work specifically on that project.

The agile and lean boards are a good visual introduction to agile: invite colleagues to stand-up meetings at your board when you need their input so that they can contribute.

Introduce the retrospective five questions format (see Section 22) into a review meeting to gain feedback and identify actions going forward.

Use the retrospective five questions in meetings:

- What has gone well?
- What can we do better?
- What is stopping us?
- What has changed?
- What is next?

Mapping work onto a board with cards/notes and tracking its progress by holding daily stand-ups and weekly review meetings helps others immediately to see work in progress and the benefits of visualising work. Once this has been established, further tools, such as estimation games, the structure of sprints and tactics such as MVP and metrics to analyse performance, can be introduced and used to help improve and refine the team's performance.

Agile is a set of building blocks that can be adapted and formed in a variety of ways to support a team. By providing a team with the agile foundations and structures, a team can easily adapt and evolve boards and communication channels that suit their particular functions and needs.

A key reason that agile tools and materials are great for teams is because they are tactile and visual. This means they are on display and not hidden away in spreadsheets and planning documents. Agile dashboards provide simple, real-time visual methods that inform both you and those with whom you work.

Adoption lifecycles

If you are planning to introduce agile across a team or an organisation, the theory of the adoption lifecycle is valuable in raising awareness of how new solutions are adopted, and how this may impact on the adoption of agile within your team or business (see Figure 24.1).

INNOVATORS

When a new solution is introduced, innovators are the first to adopt. This small first segment are strong change agents. They like to be the first to adopt new things and their driver for adoption is mostly emotional.

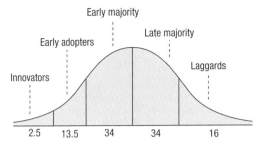

Figure 24.1   Adoption lifecycle
Source: Rogers (1995)

These adopters will provide great feedback and engage fully and they will accept solutions that are imperfect, enjoying the experimental nature of being the first to adopt the solution. Beware, however, as these adopters will be looking for the next new innovation before too long!

EARLY ADOPTERS

If innovators are the 'me first' category of adopters, then early adopters are the 'me too' category. Again, easy to convince, these adopters are keen to engage and adopt new solutions. They provide useful feedback and can help to scale, hone and refine solutions, as often they are keen to improve and develop ideas further.

EARLY MAJORITY

The early majority are a very different type to the innovators and early adopters. These adopters expect a solution that has been proven and the effects to be visible and tangible. It is likely that you will have to sell the solution to these adopters to encourage them to engage. They expect to receive a solution that is fit for purpose, and will not be so forgiving of bugs and glitches. The early majority are a good test of whether a solution is scalable and how it needs to adapt to work effectively on a larger scale.

LATE MAJORITY

The late majority are the followers. They adopt because it is perceived that everyone else has, and so they do not want to be left out. These adopters have high expectations. Based on the positive feedback that encouraged them to engage, they expect the solution to be proven and for it to be refined and perfected.

At this stage of implementation and adoption, the solution will be at maturity. Learning should be invested in identifying the next version or model of the solution that will inspire the innovators and early adopters to upgrade and sustain their engagement, ensuring that the solution does not lose traction as a preferred solution.

LAGGARDS

The final stage of adoption are the laggards: those that lag behind and are late to adopt. They are highly adverse to change and will be very difficult to convert without forced change, which can be stressful. The positive side of attracting laggards is that, by this stage, the change of solution should be well embedded with others and so become normalised, which means that laggards may inadvertently adopt the solution as it has become a familiar feature of their external environment.

Agile is a combination of tools that can be used and adopted in a variety of ways. As agile practices are established, these tools can be evolved and adapted so they are continuously tailored to suit the needs of the individual, teams and business as they grow and evolve themselves.

As well as serving as a guide to how agile may be adopted more widely, this lifecycle of adoption applies in many different situations where there is change and new solutions are emerging. It can be used to guide adoption of the solutions you develop using agile and as a guide to how you personally adopt new solutions and, more widely, how others adopting new solutions may impact upon you.

25. Agile culture

> **KEY LEARNING POINT**
>
> Identify the ways in which agile works to foster a
> healthy and positive working environment.

Agile helps to support a positive culture where shared beliefs and values
can be developed, and a shared consensus on the purpose and goals of
the team as a collective can be gained.

Regular structured feedback helps to maintain awareness and alleviates feelings of uncertainty: in delivering the outcomes expected, the team know
where they are and accept accountability together rather than as individuals.

Solution-focused

It is important for the team to adopt the agile philosophy of continuous
learning and improvement. By using agile teams can improve the accuracy
of forecasts and map out potential options more realistically. This enables
forward thinking and a solution-focused attitude within the team.

COLLABORATIVE

- Agile encourages team members to pull together to achieve a combined effort. When relationships are open this helps to build trust.

- Agile helps to bring teams together by opening up communication
  channels. With regular forums for discussion, the team are able to get
  to know each other better and begin to work together more smoothly.

- Collaborative behaviour improves the flow of work and reduces pressure on any one individual in the team.

PERFORMANCE

- Agile tools and metrics provide transparent data and tools to measure
  the performance of the team.

- When a team achieves a good rhythm and routine for working together
  this helps to create a balanced and realistic expectation of how much
  work can be achieved.

- Performance is measured for the team so the outputs become owned by the team rather than individuals. This encourages team members to help each other as there is a mutual benefit if the performance of the team improves.

- Peer review naturally occurs when discussing work ahead and reflecting on previous performance.

FLEXIBILITY

- The learn-act-reflect cycle supports a team that is open to change and provides a structure that encourages learning and development.

- The state of continuous improvement and delivery helps teams to be flexible and adjust systems to suit individual needs rather than being constrained by fixed and rigid processes and tools.

Shared purpose

The inclusive nature of agile promotes learning throughout a team by giving a clear view of goals and performance. Visually, the team can see how their work is structured and delivered and, at a glance, see what everyone is doing at any time:

- A positive, solution-focused way forward.

- Gives everyone on the team visibility of work.

- An inclusive method that gives everyone a voice.

- Empowers teams to identify and improve their work.

SHARED VALUES

The agile values in the Agile Manifesto (http://agilemanifesto.org/) and its principles outlined in Section 6 help the team to develop a shared understanding of what being agile means, and can be tailored to fit teams.

Value *individuals and interactions* over processes and tools.

Value *working solutions* over comprehensive documentation.

Value *customer collaboration* over contract negotiation.

Value *responding to change* over following a plan.

SHARED UNDERSTANDING

- Clear goals with objectives are vital to help the team to work with a common purpose.

- Brings the whole team into the decision-making process and provides them with a structure that allows them to define their own workloads and how the work is delivered.

- Ensures that everyone understands what is expected of them, and how that contributes to overall objectives and goals.

- Helps teams to focus on a specific problem and manage change on top of their day-to-day workloads.

- Results in a shared definition of success and a shared reality that help to ensure the team are all on the same page, and that a common language is used.

SHARED PERFORMANCE

- Metrics that help to track the use of resources, time and effort help to raise awareness of what the team are consuming and what value this then generates for the wider business.

- Metrics generated through the board are also valuable in order to validate, justify and evidence work that has been achieved, as well as flag problems both within the team and more widely by making them tangible and visible.

- Visual boards and collaborative tools allow logic to be mapped and for teams to see beyond the logic to discover innovative and creative opportunities for improvement.

SHARED LEARNING

The regular stand-up, planning and retrospective meetings help to ensure that the team are aware of the real-time position and work in progress, as well as the longer-term progress towards goals and outcomes, and this clarity helps to adjust and tune efforts accordingly.

Reflective meetings are key activities to help the team to understand their progress, and to identify change and challenges that the project faces. By holding regular stand-up and retrospective meetings, issues can been seen early and addressed quickly and easily. A key outcome of these meetings is learning and the sharing of experiences and progress to support future work, and implement improvements based on that learning.

Collaboration

COLLABORATIVE TOOLS

The central tool for encouraging the team to work as a unit rather than as individuals is the agile dashboard. The board gives the team a shared space for their workload, which encourages them to work collectively to find the best way to deliver the volume and quality of work required in the time available.

Collaborative activities, such as daily stand-up meetings and retrospectives, provide the team with an ongoing communications channel rather than the traditional once a month team meeting. A key feature and benefit of the agile system is that it enables teams to engage quickly and regularly within their working days rather than as a separate activity.

Estimation games and priority ranking tools for defining, estimating and prioritising work provide tools that support collaboration by facilitating communication within the team. The tools work to provide channels to discuss and communicate views of the situation openly, encouraging the team to share previous experiences and knowledge in order to assist the decision-making process. Through open discussion, expectations are clarified and a shared understanding is developed.

CONSENSUS

- Estimation planning games and priority ranking tools help the team to gain consensus and agreement.

- Communication channels allow each member of the team to contribute and have a voice.

- Experience and knowledge can be shared to identify who is best suited to which jobs and working with whom.

- Peer learning is strong, as skills are shared and developed as a by-product of working together.

- Ensures that the team does not become overly dependent on one person, which helps to mitigate losses if a team member leaves or is absent for a period of time.

COMMUNICATION

- Clear communication and visibility of jobs to do along with clear success criteria to reduce the risk of mis-communication or misunderstanding amongst the team.

- Builds relationships with customers and users and gains a deeper level of involvement and support that helps to secure the team's loyalty and buy-in to the solution.

- Short regular meetings to work on mapping, reviewing and planning enable teams to discuss and communicate openly and develop a shared understanding within the team and, more widely, with customers, suppliers and associates.

- Communication during reflection as a team is a key activity to help the team to understand their progress and to identify change and challenges that the project faces together.

COLLABORATION GAMES

There are some great games for teams to help them come together to explore scenarios and identify solutions, such as mapping timelines. Smooth sailing is a game I have used, which helps teams to identify the things that are causing friction and slowing them down, and those things that help them gain traction and work optimally. The game is adapted from Innovation Games™ Speedboat, originally developed by Luke Hohmann (http://www.innovationgames.com/).

SMOOTH SAILING

Outcomes of the game:

- Identify issues that are causing friction in the team and preventing them from achieving optimum performance.

- Identify ideas that the team have to gain traction and improve their performance.

- Achieve a shared understanding of key issues being experienced or that are expected to occur.

- Create ideas and opportunities for improvement as a team, discussing each to clarify what and why this is a sail or anchor on the boat.

- Create actionable jobs to implement improvements for the future.

Each team draws a boat on their paper, a simple sailing boat with a body, main mast and anchor. Using sticky notes, key issues that are causing friction are used as anchors and potential options for solutions are used as sails. These are then discussed and scored.

The boat represents the team or a specific project or job.

- The anchors are added to represent the things that slow the boat down, things that cause friction and delay progress or affect performance.

- Once the anchors have been added, the team should discuss and score each. With a negative score to represent the impact this anchor has on the speed and performance of the 'boat', score between –10 to –1. This should be a measure of how much this anchor slows the boat down. If it has very little impact on speed, it scores –1; if it is a significant slow-down, it scores –5; and if it comes to a complete stop, it scores –10!

- Then the sails are added. These represent the things that help the team to gain traction and speed. This can especially include ideas and opportunities to release, raise or compensate for the identified anchors.

- Again, once all the sails have been added, the team should discuss and score each with a +1 to +10 as a measure of how much this sail will speed up the boat. If it is a little better, it scores +1; if there is a significant increase in speed and performance, it scores +5; and if is full speed ahead, it scores +10!

This game helps teams to explore what they feel is holding them back and what can be done to improve performance. The key strength of the game is that it encourages communication and discussion and can lead to the identification of key actions that can help to improve the performance of the team.

Agile environment

The working environment for any team should be structured to help that team to work effectively and efficiently. The workspace for a team should be safe and comfortable and should be owned by that team, that is, in how it is set up and maintained for maximum benefit. Spaces where the team can be creative away from distractions of day-to-day activities are vital to help the focus of a team.

SHARED SPACE

- Wall space is essential to enable physical boards to be present in the team space. However, many teams I work with use corridor space, windows, room dividers, mobile whiteboards and other suitable alternatives.

- Boards in shared spaces are good as they make work even more visible to the wider business.

- Digital options are growing into viable solutions, but there is a unique value in the tangibility and tactile nature of physical boards and cards in bringing a team together to work collaboratively.

- The environment we work in can have a big impact on our ability to work: some workplaces are quiet and others are full of distractions. Subtleties such as layout and decor can directly affect the atmosphere and mood of a room and indirectly influence the behaviour of a team.

- The team boards, meetings and games within agile create a space for the team to share and work together.

- More widely, agile methods help teams to connect and share with other teams, providing a space where all can interact and engage.

- Teams that work in separate spaces can become easily disconnected, and teams that work remotely even more so. Using agile methods, such as team boards, can help connect teams and build regular channels of communication around a shared space.

26. Agile teams

KEY LEARNING POINT

Learn about how teams can use agile to work collaboratively and in harmony using agile communication practices and visualisation tools.

Agile is a collaborative methodology and empowers the team to identify, organise and manage the workload. Agile allows a team to take control and accountability for the work they deliver. The method provides a shared structure, language and platform for open communication and encourages reflection, learning and improvement as a team.

High-performing teams are a result of people working well together and harnessing the combined potential, so that they can achieve far higher performance and improved outcome than if they all worked as individuals. Agile provides a tool to help teams find the best structure and rhythm to deliver value as effectively and efficiently as possible.

A high-performing agile team is:

- highly adaptable and flexible;
- responsive to rapid change;
- highly productive and efficient;
- positive and forward thinking;
- motivated and collaborative;
- dynamic and self-organising;
- durable and strong.

An agile manager accepts that their team has the skills, knowledge and expertise to make decisions and create the best solution, based on the goal and objectives they are given. If properly implemented, the agile approach provides capacity for training and resources to support the creation of highly effective and productive teams.

Team structure

A good team structure is important to support the development of a team that is able to perform optimally. This includes its ability to communicate effectively, work together collaboratively and and deliver work efficiently.

SIZE

Agile is all about keeping things small, simple and actionable, even when scaled up for larger solutions and teams. It does this by breaking down a large scope of work into smaller packages of achievable chunks of work. Concepts such as the minimum viable product (MVP) are used to develop early solutions and deliver value early with a small amount of resources, and then scale up to expand and refine solutions as needed.

Small agile teams of 4–12 members are able to work on specific chunks of work, allowing them to focus and achieve optimum performance by maintaining a size where good communication and collaboration is still practical between members. Agile teams can maintain strong communication channels using roadmaps and pipelines to connect them, optimising flow and consistency.

ROLES

Within a team it is important to have clear roles and responsibilities so that each member is clear on what is expected from them and when. Team leaders and managers must balance skills and preferences to ensure that all work is completed.

Since agile empowers individuals to select their tasks from the defined batch of work and are encouraged to work with and support the wider team, members begin to shift their preferences towards particular tasks they are good at and enjoy.

The way that teams and their roles and responsibilities are formed can change as an agile team develops and members find their optimal positions. Agile teams are more goal-driven and project-orientated, formed from existing skills teams (for example, marketing and production). Members from across the business specialise by forming virtual cross-functional teams that contain a mixture of skills to work on a particular problem or segment of the business. Agile helps to facilitate teams that bring the right people together for the right projects.

SCRUMS

In software there is a form of agile team, which is known as a scrum (developed by Jeff Sutherland and others in the 1990s as a software development approach). In a scrum team there is typically a team leader known as the 'scrum master', a product owner that is ideally the customer, and a number of multi-discipline team members.

The team leader, or scrum master, is responsible for facilitating the team and its members. They ensure that sprint planning, stand-ups and retrospectives are scheduled and held. The team leader is responsible for generating and sharing performance and feedback metrics for review in team meetings and for sharing with wider stakeholders. A team leader ensures that resources are available to the team as needed and is responsible for dealing with blocks or problems. The team leader also ensures that new work is channelled to the team via the inbox rather than ad hoc, and that discussions are held routinely to review and build in these requests as appropriate.

The product owner is a person that represents the users and customers of the work that the team delivers. The product owner is engaged actively with the team, testing and reviewing the value and fit of the solution being developed. The role of the product owner is to provide the team with a direct link to the customer/user perspective and to help identify needs and formulate solutions. The product owner contributes through providing the customer perspective and voice at planning sessions and feedback at retrospective meetings.

Team boards

The agile team board is a mutual space for the team to share and communicate work to do and work in progress, as well as review the outcome of completed work. The board helps to manage the capacity of the team and manage how the team receives new work.

SNAPSHOT

When an agile dashboard is introduced and work in progress is captured and tracked, it enables the members to gain a snapshot of their work immediately: it gives sight of the mix of their work, and allows them to gain a perspective on the rate of work achieved and the team's wider activities. This information can provide team performance metrics that can be analysed to uncover the strengths and weaknesses of performance and the validity and effectiveness of current processes and systems.

Shared and dependent work is captured on the board. By being aware of others' workloads and their dependencies, a team can plan sprints to deliver work on demand as it is needed by others. Using estimation and planning games, the team can find a volume and order of work that allows everyone to perform and deliver as effectively as possible.

AVATARS AND SWIM LANES

Individual team members can distinguish themselves in a couple of ways to show what they are working on.

Avatars, a picture to represent a person, can be used as markers to show work in progress. Swim lanes (rows showing multiple workflows across the board) can be used to represent different people or types of work, if the team find this easier initially to visualise their workloads. Over time, a team usually will remove these swim lanes in favour of avatars and keys. As they begin to work more as a team rather than individuals, work is tailored with colours, shapes or labelling to differentiate board components.

CHANGE PROJECTS

A good way to introduce an agile dashboard is for a particular scope of work or project that the group is working on as a type of pilot. This allows the team to take a minimum viable change approach (see Section 16) that gives the opportunity to test the method on a component of work that may be low risk and convenient.

LAYOUTS

The agile dashboard structure is an effective way for teams to manage tasks or activities (see Figure 17.3). This is particularly useful if the team is working on specific projects or is responsible for producing a specific product or solution that has a number of shared or dependent activities or purposes.

CREATING LINKS

Agile dashboards can use the 'inbox' and 'done' boxes as a flag for the activity to be received by the team or passed on to another team. For example, if the work needs to be recorded onto a time-recording system for client billing, an administrator may take the completed cards and use the actual recorded time and put this into the system. Introducing a method of recording time that also provides valuable performance metrics back to the team can help to improve the recording of time, which can ensure that appropriate resources are made available and can support an increase in revenue if time spent is chargeable to clients.

Self-organising teams

Teams can choose work to do from the defined activities in that sprint of work. This means that team members can choose in which order they do their activities, both individually and as part of the team. If we find we are good at something, generally we tend to enjoy doing it. Some of us like a constant challenge, while others enjoy routine. Allowing teams to choose who and when the work is delivered encourages the team to work together and help each other to achieve. Using agile to identify where individuals are strong performers and where they enjoy working means that they can be utilised most effectively in the team: it means that there is less friction and greater acceptance when delegating and assigning tasks.

- Working as a collective, the team develop a greater understanding of who is best at what and where support is needed. Team metrics encourage working together to improve and help raise collective targets.

- The team are empowered to take accountability for getting the work done by their inclusion in the decision-making process.

- Because others' activities are visible, decisions can be made based on dependencies to help improve the flow of work and generate a better result for the team as a whole.

- Agile encourages self-organising and self-managing individuals and teams: it empowers people to make decisions and work to deliver the most appropriate solutions to meet needs and achieve established goals.

- Priorities are established through collaboration and performance analysis, gaining buy-in and better consensus among the team and its wider stakeholders.

Pairing and swarming

Since an agile team works closely together, if one area of work gets blocked or too big, team members can swarm around the problem to help alleviate the bottleneck and ensure that the flow of the team's output is maintained.

There is an approach in software development called mob programming (a team working practice developed as a practice within Extreme Programming software development teams, see Woody Zuill: http://mobprogramming.org), where the team gather around one computer to solve a specific problem or undertake a complex activity. Only one person can work at the computer at a time. The team members take turns in that position, while the other members of the team support that person, advising them on what to write, finding information out to assist them and providing feedback on their work.

Another common method used in software development is pair programming (a common practice within Extreme Programming software development teams), where two people work together on one computer to write software. One person will work on the computer while the other dictates, advises or provides research support. This method works on the theory that two heads are better than one in solving a problem. The pairing of people to work together also promotes knowledge sharing, peer learning and review.

While in some cases, boards do evoke a degree of competition – in terms of moving tasks across the board – once the initial novelty subsides and awareness is raised about how each team member is dependent on the other, this begins to cultivate a movement towards collaboration where each realises the benefit to them if their teammates are also performing well.

Transparency

In some circumstances, agile should come with a warning label, as this method literally does put the writing on the wall. In other words, it gives your work a high level of transparency. It will show visually your strengths and weaknesses, it will show up bottlenecks and problems with existing processes, it will show high and low performance, it will uncover friction and blocks.

Agile raises awareness and there is nowhere to hide, combining this visibility with a toolset that enables learning and improvement. Unfortunately, it can reveal issues in a team but, in the majority of cases, it is an enlightening experience for a team, as they use agile to identify and implement opportunities for improvement, embrace the opportunity to work more closely together and begin to see and implement improvements.

Awareness

SELF-AWARENESS

Agile approaches provide individuals with a much higher level of insight and self-awareness of their own work, and their performance against others in the team. This new level of self-awareness can stir up emotions either positively or negatively, which can affect behaviour and attitude significantly. Agile is a great tool for developing self-awareness of how we prefer to work, the highs and lows and how external and internal forces – whether professional or personal – affect our work and also our behaviour.

SELF-MANAGEMENT

Agile is a self-management tool that provides methods for supporting the management and delivery of work. The process of reflection allows each individual to review and learn from previous actions and how they affect the environment in which they work. This time allows each team member to reflect upon their own performance, and establish how they wish to perform in the future and what changes are needed next time.

SOCIAL AWARENESS

Using agile provides teams with an opportunity to achieve a higher level of social awareness. Through interaction and awareness of the work that others do, members get to know more about the people they work with, such as each member's strengths and weaknesses, their preferences, habits and the way they like to work. By using this knowledge, the team can form better working relationships, which help to streamline and improve performance.

RELATIONSHIP MANAGEMENT

Agile working highlights the dependencies and relationships within the team and raises awareness of the impact of these. The team become better aware of the internal and external behaviours and actions that affect the rhythm and morale of the team, and use agile to identify these and manage them better. The team develop an understanding of how best to communicate and manage relationships in a positive and considerate way.

Forecasting and reflection are powerful agile tools and help to manage awareness and respond in a way that is positive for the team and all of its members.

EMOTIONAL INTELLIGENCE

Together, these four insights represent our emotional intelligence and form four key skills that allow us to understand ourselves better and how to improve our work with others (see Figure 26.1). Our emotional intelligence can be developed through gaining a better awareness and understanding of our own and our colleagues' beliefs, values and behaviour and how personal dynamics and preferences impact upon performance and working relationships.

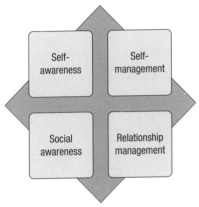

Figure 26.1 Emotional intelligence skills model
Source: Bradberry (2005)

Etiquette

It is important to establish board etiquette with a team. Clarity over the rules and expectations helps a team to develop a working relationship: for example, who can move what/where on the board. Generally, only the task owner can move their task(s).

Receiving work requests ad hoc can be very distracting, interrupting work in progress, which can cause delays. If new work is being received constantly, a team can end up starting projects but not finishing them before moving onto the next new work.

Inbound work should be placed in the inbox for review at the next stand-up or sprint planning meeting, rather than simply placed straight into to do. The reason for this control is that the work in the current sprint is fixed and at full capacity so, in order to allocate time/resources to this task in the current sprint, either something must be taken out, or the task estimated and assigned to the slack time available during the sprint.

Agile particularly works to control how new work is received and provides a channel that can be managed and reviewed regularly.

In order to be open and trusting, a degree of confidentiality and mutual respect needs to be established and shared with the team so that these rules are clear and can be adhered to.

Team performance

- The use of visual planning boards provides a physical communication space that provides real-time information on who is doing what, and gives a view to any outside body on what the team are currently working.

- Agile methods help teams to see their performance on a daily basis and provide a deeper level of metrics that allow the team to measure and improve their performance.

- Giving a team the tools to forecast and measure their performance helps to develop ownership and accountability. This helps them to become a self-managing and self-organising team.

TEAM METRICS

- Through agile practices, a team can identify where effort is needed to maintain overall performance and optimum workflow.

- Metrics gathered and analysed can help to inform the team about the accuracy between their forecast and actual performance at a number of levels.

- By estimating activities and then recording actuals the team can establish if, and what, activities are being over- or under estimated and adjust their calculations accordingly when next estimating similar work.

TEAM PRODUCTIVITY

The team can learn from the metrics on performance, such as volume, velocity and burn down rates to identifying why performance is not as expected, and look to make wider improvements: for example, improving skills through training, making changes to processes or adjusting future estimations to take account of the differences as needed.

Situations where work is being held up or slowed down can be reviewed to identify where improvements can be made, and the level of forecast work versus capacity can be measured and adjusted if needed to meet demand or manage expectations.

PEER PERFORMANCE

- From their board, the team can see the distribution of workload: high and low performers will be made visible.

- The 80:20 principle identifies where 80 per cent of value is delivered by 20 per cent of the team.

- The natural tendency of peer review supported by agile facilitation tools, such as stand-ups and retrospectives, can inspire low performers to seek development opportunities.

- High performers look for ways to improve their performance further and agile provides them with visibility of their dependencies, which they can support and improve, and this will have a positive impact on their own work. Therefore, there is mutual benefit and opportunity to develop as a team.

BOTTLENECKS AND DISTRACTIONS

The team also can see the work that does not get done and identify why this is the case. It could be that a suitable solution has been delivered with fewer resources; that there is a block or problem; that there is work the team does not particularly like doing; a skills gap, or there is just too much work and some things keep lapsing continuously.

There are a number of ratios that can be identified to see the variation of work that is being achieved. The team also can identify how much of the work is predictable, and how much work is unplanned and unexpected. If a team can predict that on average, 30 per cent of work is unplanned, then slack can be built into sprints to allow for this work.

- The team can use metrics to measure their velocity and quality of work and work together to deliver improvements.

- Bringing a team's workload together in one place can help to share work when distractions, blocks or bottlenecks occur.

- Agile boards provide a channel to working together on tasks, and raise awareness of other workloads and how one piece of work may impact upon another.

Resistance

Wherever there is change there is likely to be resistance. While early adopters will be proactive and engaged, later adopters often will come up with excuses and reasons why agile will not work for them, especially when it is first introduced.

I ALREADY KNOW WHAT I AM DOING, WHERE IS THE VALUE?

Some of us already have a good handle on what we are doing and when. We are comfortable and happy, and we do not see the point in adopting what appears to be a personal work management tool when we already have everything under control.

But does everyone else you work with know? When we work as part of a team or do something that impacts on another, then it is not just about us. Agile is a way to communicate and share. By working more closely with others and sharing our work, a team can work to improve their performance collectively.

WE DEVELOP HUNDREDS OF PRODUCTS A YEAR WITH HUNDREDS OF PEOPLE: IT WILL NOT WORK FOR US

All the more need for agility then, surely? Yes, true, it would be an overwhelming board if the entire business were mapped out using sticky notes, and it would require a large amount of wall space, but that, generally, is not required. Agile is about change and improvement and chunks of focused activity, not everything and anything that can be mapped. Many businesses have adopted agile within parts of the business where it can be used to identify and resolve problems and identify routes to growth.

IT SOUNDS A BIT LIKE LETTING GO OF THE STEERING WHEEL, WE HAVE TO HAVE A PLAN

Agile does have planning and it does have goals. It is not about forgetting what we already know and plan to do; it is accepting that probably we do not know it all and there are likely to be a few things that change along the way.

Agile as a methodology helps to change direction without having to descend into chaos because it takes account for the fact that there will be change. Agile is a great tool for managing the unknown. Lean is a great tool for refining and improving systems and processes. It is not about replacing current approaches, systems and tools, it is a method for improving them.

I AM NOT ALWAYS AT MY DESK AND MY TEAM WORK REMOTELY

There are now a number of digital solutions available to create agile boards digitally for sharing. Agile does not have to be at your side night and day; it can be visited daily or even weekly. If the team are distributed, then it can help to bring them together virtually. A key issue with distributed teams is that they find communication a barrier, and agile can provide a suite of tools to help at least lessen the impact of remote working. Video conferencing and remote file sharing make it possible to use parts of agile to provide a fixed shared space when everything else is constantly moving.

CUSTOMERS WANT TO FIX THE SOLUTION AT THE START

You can point out that customers do not know exactly what they want at the start by using agile to help them explore their goals, the reality and the options. Despite this recurring fear that customers will not accept a solution without a definitive price, scope and time, they will when it has been tried. Agile works to build trust and awareness with the customer. It includes them in the decision-making process, delivers value early and allows them to change their mind. Ask your clients, would they like to fix the solution now, or would they like the option to change their mind along the way. You may or may not be surprised to hear they would like the option to change their mind when you ask them directly.

27. Lean teams

KEY LEARNING POINT

Establish collaborative working and connect teams using visualisation of workflows.

A lean pipeline dashboard is useful to help gain visibility of the pipeline of work that is being undertaken by the team or teams towards a shared goal. The pipeline helps teams to pass jobs, projects and customers between one another, share information and resources between each other and work collaboratively to create an efficient and productive workflow at a higher level in the business. The dashboard helps the team to see the flow of work through the pipeline: it gives a view of the stages prior to and following their own, and raises awareness of these related and dependent stages.

Running a business effectively and efficiently while pushing forward with growth plans can be a difficult balance. As volume of work increases, existing processes and systems used to manage the workload may not sustain the higher volumes effectively. Mapping and monitoring pipelines such as the customer journey can help teams to sustain workflow as it increases by highlighting blocks and issues as they evolve.

- A lean workflow board can work very well to help the team to work collectively in passing work between each other.

- Boards help to raise awareness by allowing the teams to see where work is in the pipeline, what work is soon to reach them, and what progress has been made on work they have passed along.

A pipeline board is a simple way to represent the flow, volume and velocity of work travelling through the business. Depending on the type of work being undertaken, clients, projects, jobs or products are represented on cards and their status tracked on a pipeline broken down into various relevant stages.

- Regular stand-up and retrospective meetings are held around the board to discuss the status of work, update the board and hand over work to the next stage.

- Within each stage the card can be in four states – to do, doing, done or waiting to show its status.

- Visual representations of pipelines help teams to see the status of work, where there are bottlenecks and delays in the process and how to evolve the pipeline to be more productive and efficient.

- Optimum and maximum capacities can be identified by measuring the throughput of work to find the optimum speed and volume that can be processed efficiently, while maintaining quality outputs and happy teams.

- Lean efficiencies (Section 19) can be analysed to identify ways to change and improve the pipeline by removing waste, reallocating talent and ensuring that workflow is optimised.

Customer journey

The customer pipeline in Figure 27.1 shows a client's journey through a business. Each card represents a client and their position and status within the pipeline.

On this customer pipeline board we can see that there are a lot of prospects in progress but work seems to be blocked at the quotation stage. This might be where there is a delay in receiving feedback from the potential customers and converting the quote into a contractual agreement.

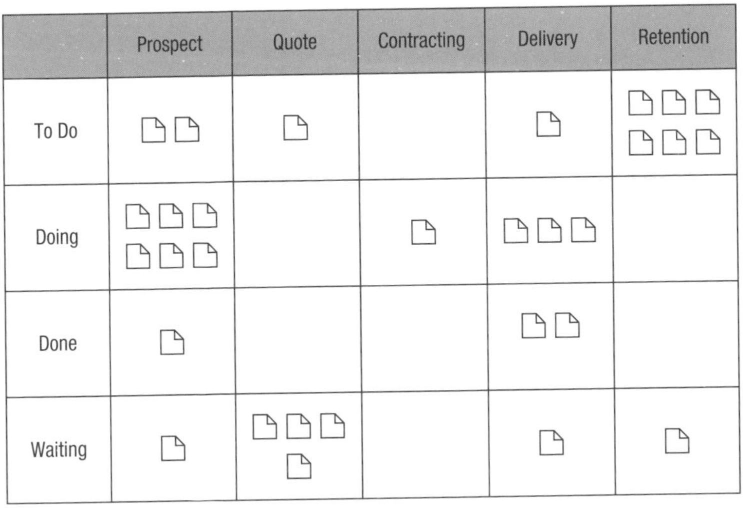

	Prospect	Quote	Contracting	Delivery	Retention
To Do	▯ ▯	▯		▯	▯ ▯ ▯ ▯ ▯ ▯
Doing	▯ ▯ ▯ ▯ ▯ ▯		▯	▯ ▯ ▯	
Done	▯			▯ ▯	
Waiting	▯	▯ ▯ ▯ ▯		▯	▯

Figure 27.1   New customer lean pipeline

There is only one contract in progress but the delivery stage is currently busy.

Looking forward, the teams may find that there is a lack of work to deliver if the quotes are not unblocked and converted into contracts, or prospects convert quickly, which would leave the delivery team with capacity to spare. This is a good example of where the team can swarm around the blocked quotes and future leads to help convert them into contracted work.

There also appears to be a backlog of work to be actioned in the retention stage. This may be because the team are currently concentrating their efforts on generating new prospects, or it could be that customer retention is a weakness in the pipeline and is not being actioned or managed appropriately.

Enabling teams to work throughout the pipeline helps to develop teams that are multi-skilled and understand the phases that occur before and after their work. This helps to raise awareness and appreciation of how their actions are related to and impact upon others' work.

This physical visual representation of a pipeline can become difficult if there is a large volume of projects, clients or products in progress. In this instance, the board can be used to focus in on specific areas or show work at a higher level. For example, the board might focus on a specific market segment or new products in development.

28. Agile leadership

> **KEY LEARNING POINT**
>
> Explore how agile methods support the development of a shared and common purpose within a business, breaking down barriers and improving communication throughout the business.

Agile can be used as a leadership and management tool to support and maintain successful organisations faced with constant change in an ever-complex and unforgiving global economy.

The direction of a business is governed by its capacity and capabilities. The role of a leadership within a business is to provide the business with a shared sense of purpose through clear goals and objectives that provide the team with clear direction for the long and short term.

- Agile methods direct and manage business activities to ensure that there are sufficient resources and capacity to attract and fulfil demand for its business services in a profitable and sustainable way.

- Good leadership and decision making should include being informed by the people working within the business. Performance metrics of the business should inform the business strategy, direction and any change and growth plans.

- Agile provides a tool to help communication work both ways within the organisation. It provides tools to enable key information to be fed back to management and leadership teams, so that they can reflect and learn from it, in order to inform the future direction.

Using the GROW coaching model described in Section 8 (see Figure 8.1), business leaders can work collaboratively to establish goals and objectives with their teams.

- Agile establishes a shared language and understanding across the business, which helps to ensure key messages are communicated and understood. Key values and beliefs are established and shared to focus on specific objectives and to encourage innovation and collaboration.

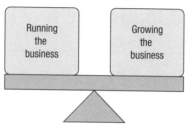

Figure 28.1   Balancing running and growing

- Agile helps to break down barriers and provides a way of working that allows all layers of an organisation to see work in progress at various levels and how they are inter related.

- Agile is a way of working that empowers teams and individuals with the freedom to work and be clear about their role and responsibilities, enabling them to see how their work contributes to the overall goal, and where dependencies lie.

Directing change

Leaders and managers are challenged to balance running an efficient and effective business with growing and scaling the business through change and improvement (see Figure 28.1).

As a business grows, the workings of the business must grow and evolve to manage increasing volumes of workload most efficiently. Agile provides an approach and structure to manage a busy team and help the team to:

- Be responsive to visual cues and flags that agile boards highlight.

- Recognise where change is needed, due to blocks, distractions or barriers to performance or development.

- Evidence the need for change and improvement through metrics and measures.

- Prioritise and control the amount of change to balance against existing workload.

- Identify trends and events that affect the business.

- Ensure quality is maintained by making certain that teams are not over-committing, by measuring and controlling workload.

Breaking down barriers

- Poor communication and misunderstanding are key reasons for friction and disconnect between teams. As a communication management tool, agile provides a simple and practical way for teams to communicate and share their work across the business.

- Agile tools and materials are tactile and visual. This means they are on display and not hidden away in spreadsheets and planning documents.

- Agile enables communication to flow both up and down through the business to provide clarity and transparency. Agile helps to break down the barriers of hierarchy within a business by providing a shared space where leaders and managers can communicate and understand the reality of day-to-day working within the business and what is going on.

 ## Strategic roadmap

Businesses first and foremost provide products and services, and these need to evolve constantly in order to keep pace with today's changing and developing markets. A strategic roadmap (a tool adapted from Jeff Brantley's keynote speech at the Agile on Beach Conference 2012 - see Brantley (2012)) helps to guide direction and balance running the business with changing and growing the business.

A roadmap (see Figure 28.2) helps to show the way forward for the growth and development of the business and how this breaks down into chunks of work. The roadmap shows, at a high level, the goals and milestones for the expected development of the business. It shows the multiple workflows of the products, services and resources planned for the current period and the following two to three periods, which may be quarterly, monthly or weekly, depending on the pace, type and current status of business.

While agile sprint boards and lean pipelines are used by individuals and teams to manage and visualise short-term work in progress, a strategic business roadmap is valuable to forecast activities at a high level over the medium term, to align teams and activities being undertaken across the business.

The roadmap links into agile dashboards that provide details on the current work in progress, and maps the future work into the backlog of work to be actioned during later sprints of work.

	July	August	September	October	November
Goal/milestones	📄📄	📄📄	📄📄	📄📄	📄📄
Research and development	📄📄📄	📄	📄	📄📄📄	📄
Marketing	📄	📄📄📄	📄📄	📄	📄📄📄
Sales	📄	📄📄	📄📄📄	📄📄	📄
Production and delivery	📄📄	📄📄	📄📄	📄📄📄	📄📄📄
Resources/infrastructure	📄	📄	📄📄	📄📄	📄📄📄
Trends/events	📄	📄📄	📄	📄📄	📄📄📄

Figure 28.2   Example of a business roadmap

By mapping work onto a roadmap at a higher level, gaps can be identified where slack is available to schedule growth and projects at optimum times, show gaps where new business could be gained, or where work can be taken from busier periods and moved to quieter ones.

- Goals/milestones could show the launch of new products, key project dates, delivery dates or objectives of the business over a rolling time period.

- Key areas of business activity are shown on the board: for example research and development may show new products in development, while marketing may show key marketing campaigns to promote these new products, and production and delivery may show the anticipated production of the new product.

- Significant changes and variations to resources and infrastructure are shown on the roadmap to raise awareness and help to ensure that these changes align well with business activities. For example, this could be a new systems implementation, recruitment of new personnel or an office move.

- Trends and events show key dates and times for the business, trade shows, peak season, trips, holiday and other events that affect the capacity or capability of the team.

Information on the roadmap can be differentiated with colours and labelling to help show areas of activity. It should be updated regularly by the management team and available to teams to view at any time.

A roadmap helps teams to identify dependencies and see what other teams are doing. Raising the awareness of cross-team dependencies can help form links and collaborative activity between the teams to achieve the best flow and find ways to improve, streamline and scale.

This type of roadmap gives a high-level view of the activity of the team over a period of time. It also helps to show where capacity, such as people and resources, will be stretched during busy periods, and underutilised at other, quieter times. This is due often to seasonal or market trends: for example, a seaside hotel will be at maximum capacity during the summer months, but verge on empty during January, due to the nature of when people generally choose to take holidays by the sea.

The benefit of a visual roadmap is that all teams can see how their work fits into the wider business context. It allows key information to be displayed and provides a view of the routes to be taken to fulfil business goals and guide direction.

29. Agile management

> **KEY LEARNING POINT**
>
> Learn how to use agile as a tool to improve team performance and individual job satisfaction.

As a management tool, agile enables matching of the capacity and capabilities of the business to the goals and objectives for the business going forward. Agile tools and methods help to coordinate the work to be done into projects and activities for current and future action.

Agile provides a real-time snapshot of work in progress and, over time, metrics to measure performance of key components of the business, such as its products, services, people, systems and processes.

Agile can be used to help solve workflow problems and identify why it is happening, such as resource issues, an issue with the process or system, a lack of skills or inaccurate estimations.

Workflow management

Workflow management is vital is to ensure that there is the capacity and capability within the team and to ensure that external dependencies, such as materials or budget, are available to support the team's optimum performance. Management teams can use agile tools to work within their teams in order to identify changes that will improve capacity and capabilities, such as improvements to systems and processes.

Continuous flow of work can be overwhelming for a team, especially if opportunities for work exceed the capacity of the team. Backlogs of work can build and work can be left unfinished as new priorities arise or situations change. Teams often underestimate the time needed to complete work, especially if it is new and unknown and, if deadlines are unachievable, then they lose their potency. Unrealistic pressure on a team to overperform can lead to corners being cut, quality suffering and wastage increasing.

Agile helps to organise and prioritise the backlog of work to be dealt with alongside new work and change projects. It helps cut projects that are no longer viable, finish off incomplete work and park future work for later consideration.

Agile is an approach that supports the development of good working relationships and better understanding across teams to help identify collaborative opportunities for improvement.

- As a manager, it is easy to see by reviewing the board what work has been completed, what is currently in progress and what is yet to be completed without interrupting the team.

- Workflows are connected, coordinated and visible to all, which helps to raise awareness across teams.

- Estimation and ranking tools can be used to define, agree and prioritise work with teams and create metrics to measure performance.

- Sprints of work with stand-up meetings and retrospectives provide time for the team to reflect and learn in order to inform their future activities, and feed back to management on progress and performance.

Workload management

- Predictable and planned workload is managed by the team and guided by the team leader or manager, to ensure that time boxes align with current goals and milestones as well as the wider business activities.

- The amount of work that can be achieved can be forecast using previous performance data. The metrics delivered through agile provide information to identify and implement improvements and provide insights to identify future improvement opportunities.

- Slack can be built into sprints of work for potential ad hoc work expected and for change and improvement projects, the balance of which will be dependent on current trends, performance and priority.

- Continuous improvement is managed through rapid daily stand-ups, and review and learning are facilitated through regular structured retrospectives and sprint planning meetings.

- Structuring work into sprints using minimum viable propositions helps to ensure that work is controlled in the short term, but is more flexible in the longer term.

- Daily stand-up meetings ensure that the teams update and review the boards continuously, and regular retrospective meetings ensure that time is given to reflect and reposition work as changes occur.

- Time to reflect and learn on what is working well and what can be done better can be provided to management to review their approach, identify change and inform the decision-making process.

Self-managing teams

- Agile methods provide a structure to define and delegate work in a way that empowers the team and individuals to be self-managing and self-organising. Teams are able to choose the work they carry out and so can select the work they do best and enjoy most.

- An empowered team will select work based on their personal preferences as well as maintain a contribution to general team activities and performance. It builds knowledge of others' work through the encouragement of working practices such as pairing and swarming, particularly during times of change.

- Agile helps to uncover and take advantage of the knowledge and skills of individuals within teams. Agile practices help to facilitate the sharing of knowledge and skills to help maintain a team that is not overly dependent on one person.

- By using boards to track a team's workflow, it enables them to take ownership of work; it provides a way to see quickly how time is being spent and a way to see opportunities for improvement.

- Metrics on team and individual progress can help when appraising work and help to identify opportunities for improving performance, such as training or ensuring that appropriate levels of support and resources are provided. For example, if work becomes blocked, the individual working on the task will move it to the waiting area of the board. During the stand-up meeting, the team can flag up that this action is needed by another party to enable their team to continue to work. For example, they may be waiting on information that the manager is able to chase up more easily than they are.

- The team leader and product owner can use performance metrics to feed back to management and the wider business to inform them of progress and influence actions, to help optimise the team's performance and address any key blocks, bottlenecks or factors that are holding them back.

- As work is completed, actual metrics deliver new insights at a team and individual level, which gives continuous feedback, providing an opportunity for continuous appraisal that recognises and celebrates success and brings development opportunities to attention.

People management

Agile is a valuable tool for helping to identify the right work to do and the right people to do it. The methodology encourages learning and development, which works to improve team and individual performance. Agile can be used to:

- Create communication channels that help to build relationships, maintain a shared understanding of the work to be done and a clear vision of the goals and objectives by which that work is driven.

- Provide feedback on individual and team performance at a variety of levels.

- Gain a better understanding of individual skills, knowledge, experience and preferences so the business can capitalise on team strengths and identify personal development opportunities.

- Identify and remove barriers and blocks that put pressure on the team and cause stress.

- Promote a positive environment that is solution-focused and action-driven to provide the optimum working environment.

Performance management

As well as a personal performance management tool, agile metrics can be used by management to identify how much work each individual contributes. This insight is valuable for managing future work delegation and identifying risks, such as the impact of the loss of a key team member.

Agile as a team tool encourages everyone to help each other to achieve a result and perform as a team. As a manager, encouraging practices such as pairing up can help to build the strength of the team, as knowledge and experience is shared among the team.

Agile should help to identify the skills gaps and needs of the team and it provides ways to build in learning and development to the culture. Personal development becomes a part of day-to-day work as agile planning ensures there are resources and time to improve and grow continually:

- Gain a better understanding of the knowledge, skills and experience within the team.

- Enable people to develop into roles they enjoy and in which they perform well.

- Establish clear expectations, such as timings, definitions and success criteria, for jobs to be completed.

- Manage allocation of work to teams and individuals through sprints to focus and guide the direction and variety of work required.

- Gain the insight of the team into best practice through facilitated communication and discussion.

- Drive better performance through looking at what can be done to improve upon previous performance.

- Ensure the right people are assigned to the right jobs.

- Set a standard of performance, so teams are clear on expectations and their targets.

- Develop awareness of selves' and others' preferences and values to build better working relationships.

- Easily pick up and reassign work when staff changes occur, bring new team members up to speed quickly and manage the migration of workload when staff exit.

- Install a culture of ongoing appraisal and review with individuals to enable continuous career and professional development, to benefit individuals and the organisation as a whole.

30. Business agility

If agile is used throughout an organisation, it creates a visual real-time model of the business's strategy, plans, journeys and day-to-day operations. The visual aids help to communicate and share information throughout the workforce and create a culture that promotes working collectively and productively.

The activities of the business are visible to all and show the team where they fit in, delivering value and sustaining the business, and how the business is structured. This can help to educate staff on the bigger picture of how their work fits into the organisation as a whole. Agile methods can be used throughout the business to promote wider business agility.

By adopting agile throughout a business, using a business roadmap, lean pipelines and agile dashboards, an organisation can communicate effectively the vision, the model, the objectives and the tactics for growth and development (see Figure 30.1). The information and transparency that agile

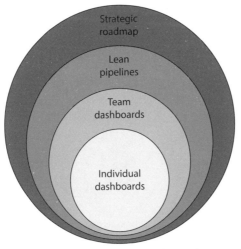

Figure 30.1   Business agility boards

produces provide insights into the effectiveness of strategies. These insights can be used to guide the direction of the business, and refine and develop its business model to ensure sustainable growth and success are achieved.

At the highest level, the road map sets outs a rolling timeline forecast for future key milestones, goals, delivery expectations and associated trends, events and rhythms.

Lean pipelines show the stages of key business processes, such as production, new product development, customer journeys or change projects. The pipeline shows a real-time status and the flow of work from one stage to another within the business. At an organisational level, these pipelines connect teams and manage the transfer of work between them, helping to optimise business performance.

For stages of work or specific projects, more detailed agile dashboards represent the current and future workload of an individual or team. At this level, boards contain actionable tasks to complete and team performance metrics.

A business can form a series of interlocking boards that facilitate the handover of work at a more detailed level between teams, guided by the higher-level pipeline and roadmap.

The metrics from each board provide feedback on the productivity and capacity of the organisation, which can help to formulate business strategy and direction and empower individuals to contribute to decision making, and improve the overall agility of the business (see Figure 30.2).

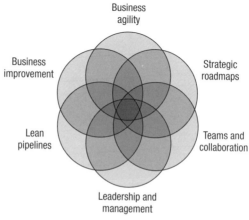

Figure 30.2   Business agility

- **Business agility** – the state achieved when a business adopts agile methods and tools to visualise business direction, delivery pipelines and activity dashboards, providing a flexible and adaptable model for business planning, delivery and change management.

- **Strategic roadmaps** – providing a businesswide roadmap that communicates and provides a high-level timeline of high-level future goals, activities, projects and trends across the organisation.

- **Teams and collaboration** – as a practical set of empowering and collaborative methods and tools to manage the delivery of work, and provide insights to guide performance and improvements.

- **Leadership and management** – as a communication and performance model to provide insights to guide business direction and strategy. A tool to help teams to work collaboratively and efficiently towards a shared and common goal. A method to balance running the business efficiently with business growth goals.

- **Lean pipelines** – models and structures for mapping journeys and running the day-to-day business, using pipelines to provide a flexible strategy and plan for the delivery of products and services to customers.

- **Business improvement** – to support the growth journey of the business and help to sustain its competitive edge. This could include the use of agile for new product or service development, improvement of business systems and processes to streamline operations or improving the culture and teams within the business.

Adopting an agile mindset and utilising agile methods at an individual level raises a person's self-awareness, increases productivity and performance, and empowers them to achieve personal career and professional development goals. When agile professionals work collectively using agile practices and thinking, in my experience the results speak for themselves. Agile helps to improve the value of the work delivered, increases satisfaction for the team and the customer, and create more harmonious and happier working environments.

The contents of this book represent an interpretation, adaption and translation from agile in software to agile in business. The cases, while anonymised and generalised, are examples of situations I have experienced in a number of different businesses through my experience working with them. Throughout the book I have given references, sources and information on some of the terms, practices and tools included in the book so you can explore them further.

FURTHER INFORMATION

Please visit the following for more information:

www.beingagileinbusiness.co.uk
Twitter@belindawaldock

What did you think of this book?

We're really keen to hear from you about this book, so that we can make our publishing even better.

Please log on to the following website and leave us your feedback.

It will only take a few minutes and your thoughts are invaluable to us.

www.pearsoned.co.uk/bookfeedback

BIBLIOGRAPHY

Agile Manifesto (2001) 'Manifesto for Agile Software Development" from www.agilemanifesto.org/principles, accessed 16/3/15.

Bell, T.E. and Thayer, T.A. 'Software requirements: Are they really a problem?', ICSE 1976 Proceedings of the 2nd International Conference on Software Engineering, pp. 61–8, Los Alamitos, CA: IEEE Computer Society Press.

Bradberry, T. (2005) *The Emotional Intelligence Quickbook*. Fireside.

Brantley, J. (2012) Keynote speech 'Agile roadmapping for fun and profit' at the Agile on the Beach Conference, 2012, www.agileonthebeach.com.

Cameron, W.B. (1963) *Informal Sociology: A Casual Introduction to Sociological Thinking*. New York: Random House.

Covey, S. (1989) 7 *Habits of Highly Effective People, Simon & Schuster*, USA

Davis, R. and Sedley, L. (2009) *Agile Coaching*. Pragmatic Bookshelf.

Humble, J. and Farley, D. (2010) *Continuous Delivery: Reliable Software Releases Through Build, Test, and Deployment Automation*. Addison Wesley.

Kelly, A. (2008) *Changing Software Development: Learning to be Agile*. John Wiley & Sons.

Kelly, A. (2012) *Business Patterns for Software Developers*. John Wiley & Sons.

Kelly, A. (2014) *Xanpan, Team Centric Agile Software Development*. Software Strategy Ltd. www.allankelly.net

Lewis, J. 'Building the Millennium Falcon – Lean and Lego', presentation at 'Agile on the Beach 2011', http://agileonthebeach.com/2011-2/2011-video/.

Megginson, L.C. (1963) 'Lessons from Europe for American Business', *The Southwestern Social Science Quarterly*, Vol. 44, No. 1.

Moore, G.A. (1999) *Crossing the Chasm*. Capstone Publishing.

Oxford Innovation Services Ltd (2012) 'Grow Cornwall Agile Programme'. Research by PFA Research Ltd, funded by the European Regional Development Fund.

Passmore, J. (2006) *Excellence in Coaching: The Industry Guide*. Kogan Page.

Poppendieck, M. and Poppendieck, T. (2003) *Lean Software Development: An Agile Toolkit*. Addison Wesley.

Poppendieck, M. 'First build the right thing, then build the thing right', Keynote speech, 'Agile on the Beach Conference 2011', http://www.slideshare.net/AgileOnTheBeach/first-build-the-right-thing.

Project Management Institute (2012) 'PMI's Pulse of the Profession In-depth Report: Organisational Agility'. Retrieved October 2014 from: http://www.pmi.org/~/media/PDF/Research/Organizational-Agility-In-Depth-Report.ashx.

Ries, E. (2011) *The Lean Startup: How Constant Innovation Creates Radically Successful Businesses*. Portfolio Penguin.

Rogers, E. (1995) *Diffusion of Innovation*, 5th ed., The Free Press, Simon & Schuster, USA

Womack, J.P, Jones, D.T. and Roos, D. (2007) *The Machine that Changed the World: The Story of Lean Production – Today's Secret Weapon in the Global Car Wars That is now Revolutionizing World Industry*. Free Press.

See also Mike Cusumano at MIT Sloan School of Management for lean software as an example of lean product development or knowledge-based produce development.

INDEX